TRADITIONAL
TATTING

Dover Publications, Inc., New York

Published in Canada by General Publishing Company, Ltd., 30 Lesmill Road, Don Mills, Toronto, Ontario.

Published in the United Kingdom by Constable and Company, Ltd.

This Dover edition, first published in 1986, is a new selection of patterns from *Crochet and Tatting: Heirloom Edition, Star Book No. 66*, published by the American Thread Company in 1949; *Star Book of Doilies, Book 22*, published by the American Thread Company, n.d.; *Tatted & Crocheted Designs, Star Book 30*, published by the American Thread Company in 1944; *Fine Crochet and Tatting, Book No. 259*, published by The Spool Cotton Company in 1949; *The Tatting Book, Book 111*, published by The Spool Cotton Company in 1938; *Tatting, Book No. 229*, published by The Spool Cotton Company in 1946; and *New Table Designs, Star Book No. 49*, published by the American Thread Company in 1946. A new introduction has been written specially for this edition.

Manufactured in the United States of America
Dover Publications, Inc., 31 East 2nd Street, Mineola, N.Y. 11501

Library of Congress Cataloging in Publication Data
Main entry under title:

Traditional tatting patterns.

A collection of tatting patterns from thread company leaflets of the first half of the 20th century.
1. Tatting—Patterns.   I. Weiss, Rita.
TT840.T73   1986   746.43′6041   85-27367
ISBN 0-486-25066-0 (pbk.)

Introduction

Tatting is actually very simple because there are very few stitches to learn. It was originally developed during the seventeenth century as an easy way of reproducing "knotted laces." Knotted lace was made over a cord with a netting needle. Tatting stitches are actually made over a thread, the thread being wound upon a shuttle small enough to permit its passage back and forth under the thread where the stitches are being made.

All stitches used in tatting are explained on pages 46 and 47. The stitches (or knots) and loops (or picots) are drawn up into circles or semicircles; different arrangements of these figures create different patterns. Once completed, a tatted article is very strong. Unlike knitting or crocheting, in which each stitch is dependent upon its neighbor (one loose stitch can lead to the unraveling of the project), each tatting stitch can stand alone and is difficult to undo once it has been made.

This book is a collection of some beautiful tatting designs published in instruction brochures produced by America's thread companies during the first half of this century. During that period the large thread companies produced hundreds of leaflets solely as a method of merchandising thread. Today these leaflets with their magnificent designs and instructions have become sought-after collector's items.

Modern technology now permits us to reproduce these instructions exactly as they appeared in those original leaflets many years ago. Many of the threads listed with the patterns are still available. If not, other threads that will produce comparable results are available. Check with your local needlework shop or department. Whatever type of thread you decide to use, be certain to buy sufficient thread of the same dye lot to complete the project you wish to make. It is often impossible to match shades later as dye lots vary.

When you have completed your project, it should be washed and blocked. No matter how carefully you have worked, blocking will give your tatting a more "professional" look. Use a good neutral soap or detergent and make suds in cool water. Wash by squeezing the suds through the project, but do not rub. Rinse two or three times in clear water. Starching the project will give it a crisper look. Using rustproof pins, pin the article right side down on a well-padded surface. Be sure to pin out all picots, loops, scallops, etc. When the project is almost completely dry, press through a damp cloth with a moderately hot iron. Do not rest the iron on the decorative, raised stitches. Let the steam do the work! When thoroughly dry, remove the pins.

4

Party-Time Doilies

**Materials Required: AMERICAN THREAD COMPANY "STAR"
MERCERIZED CROCHET COTTON, Article 20, Size 30, White
or Colors, 4 balls, or
"GEM" MERCERIZED CROCHET COTTON, Article 35, Size 30,
White or Colors, 3 balls.**

1 Round Doily 20 inches in diameter
1 Plate Doily 12 inches in diameter
1 Bread and Butter Doily 5½ inches in diameter
1 Tumbler Doily 4½ inches in diameter

1 Shuttle and Ball.
Plate Doily.
CENTER RING—R, 2 d, 8 p sep by 3 d, 1 d, cl r, tie and cut.
1st Row—R, 3 d, p, 3 d, join to p of center r, 3 d, p, 3 d, cl r, turn. * Ch, 4 d, 3 p sep by 4 d, 4 d, turn. R, 3 d, join to last p of last r made, 3 d, join to next p of center r, 3 d, p, 3 d, cl r, turn. Repeat from * 6 times joining last r to 1st r. Ch, 4 d, 3 p sep by 4 d, 4 d, tie and cut.
2nd Row, 1st Motif—* R, 6 d, 5 p sep by 2 d, 6 d, cl r. R, 6 d, join to last p of last r made, 2 d, p, 2 d, 4 p sep by 2 d, 6 d, cl r. Repeat from * once, tie and cut.
2nd Motif—R, 6 d, 5 p sep by 2 d, 6 d, cl r. R, 6 d, join to last p of last r made, 2 d, p, 2 d, join to corresponding p of 1st motif, 2 d, join to center p of ch of 1st row, 2 d, p, 6 d, cl r. R, 6 d, p, 2 d, join to center p of next ch of 1st row, 2 d, 3 p sep by 2 d, 6 d, cl r. R, 6 d, join to last p of last r made, 2 d, 4 p sep by 2 d, 6 d, cl r, tie and cut. Join all motifs together in same manner joining every other motif to 1st row (8 motifs).
3rd Row—R, 4 d, p, 4 d, join to 3rd free p of motif of 2nd row, 4 d, p, 4 d, cl r, turn. Ch, 8 d, 3 p sep by 4 d, 8 d, turn. R, 4 d, p, 4 d, join to 2nd free p of next r of same motif, 4 d, p, 4 d, cl r, turn. Ch, 8 d, 3 p sep by 4 d, 8 d, turn. Repeat from beginning all around, tie and cut.
4th Row—R, 1 d, 5 p sep by 1 d, 1 d, join to center p of ch of 3rd row, 1 d, 5 p sep by 1 d, 1 d, cl r, turn. * Ch, 8 d, 5 p sep by 4 d, 8 d, turn. R, 1 d, 5 p sep by 1 d, 1 d, join to center p of next ch of previous row, 1 d, 5 p sep by 1 d, 1 d, cl r, turn. Repeat from * all around. Ch, 8 d, 5 p sep by 4 d, 8 d, tie and cut.
5th Row—R, 4 d, p, 4 d, join to center p of ch of 4th row, 4 d, p, 4 d, cl r, turn. Ch, 8 d, 3 p sep by 4 d, 8 d, turn. R, 4 d, p, 4 d, join to last p of same ch of 4th row, 6 d, join to 1st p of next ch of 4th row, 4 d, p, 4 d, cl r, turn. Ch, 8 d, 3 p sep by 4 d, 8 d, turn. Repeat from beginning all around, tie and cut.
6th Row—Repeat the 4th row joining to the 5th row instead of 3rd row.
7th Row—R, 6 d, 5 p sep by 2 d, 6 d, cl r. R, 6 d, join to last p of last r made, 2 d, 2 p sep by 2 d, join to 4th p of ch of 6th row, 2 d, p, 6 d, cl r. R, 6 d, p, 2 d, join to 2nd p of next ch of 6th row, 2 d, 3 p sep by 2 d, 6 d, cl r. R, 6 d, join to last p of last r made, 2 d, 4 p sep by 2 d, 6 d, cl r, tie and cut. R, 6 d, 5 p sep by 2 d, 6 d, cl r. R, 6 d, join to last p of last r made, 2 d, p, 2 d, join to 2nd free p of previous motif, 2 d, skip 1 p, join in next p of same ch of 6th row, 2 d, p, 6 d, cl r. R, 6 d, p, 2 d, join to 2nd p of next ch of 6th row, 2 d, 3 p sep by 2 d, 6 d, cl r. R, 6 d, join to last p of last r, 2 d, 4 p sep by 2 d, 6 d, cl r, tie and cut. Join all motifs in same manner.
8th Row—R, 4 d, p, 4 d, join to 4th free p of 1 r of motif

of previous row, 4 d, p, 4 d, cl r, turn. Ch, 8 d, 3 p sep by 4 d, 8 d, turn. R, 4 d, p, 4 d, join to 1st p of next r of same motif of 7th row, 4 d, p, 4 d, cl r, turn. Ch, 8 d, 3 p sep by 4 d, 8 d, turn. Repeat from beginning all around, tie and cut.
9th Row—R, 1 d, 5 p sep by 1 d, 1 d, join to center p of ch of previous row, 1 d, 5 p sep by 1 d, 1 d, cl r, turn. Ch, 8 d, 3 p sep by 4 d, 8 d, turn. * R, 1 d, 5 p sep by 1 d, 1 d, join to center p of next ch of 8th row, 1 d, 5 p sep by 1 d, 1 d, cl r, turn. Ch, 8 d, 3 p sep by 4 d, 8 d, turn. Repeat from * all around, tie and cut.
10th Row—R, 2 d, 5 p sep by 2 d, 2 d, cl r, turn. Ch, 2 d, 2 p sep by 2 d, 2 d, join to center p of ch of 9th row, 2 d, 2 p sep by 2 d, 2 d, turn. R, 2 d, 5 p sep by 2 d, 2 d, cl r, turn. ** Ch, 2 d, 2 p sep by 2 d, 2 d, join to center p of next ch of 9th row, 2 d, 2 p sep by 2 d, 2 d, turn. R, 2 d, 5 p sep by 2 d, 2 d, cl r, turn. Ch, 2 d, 2 p sep by 2 d, 2 d, join to 4th p of opposite r, 2 d, 2 p sep by 2 d, 2 d, turn. * R, 2 d, p, 2 d, join to 4th p of last r made, 2 d, 3 p sep by 2 d, 2 d, cl r, turn. Ch, 2 d, 5 p sep by 2 d, 2 d, turn. Repeat from * 3 times. R, 2 d, p, 2 d, join to 4th p of last r made, 2 d, p, 2 d, join to 2nd p of opposite r, 2 d, p, 2 d, cl r, turn. Ch, 2 d, 2 p sep by 2 d, 2 d, join to center p of next ch of 9th row, 2 d, 2 p sep by 2 d, 2 d, turn. R, 2 d, p, 2 d, join to center p of opposite ch, 2 d, 3 p sep by 2 d, 2 d, cl r, turn.
Repeat from ** all around joining row to correspond, tie and cut.

LARGE DOILY

Work center ring, then work 10 rows same as plate doily.
11th Row—R, 6 d, p, 6 d, cl r. R, 6 d, join to center p of 3rd free p of 10th row, 6 d, join to center p of 1st free ch of next scallop, 6 d, cl r, tie and cut. Repeat from beginning all around.
12th Row—R, 3 d, 2 p sep by 3 d, 3 d, join to center p of free ch of 10th row, 3 d, 2 p sep by 3 d, 3 d, cl r, turn. Ch, 8 d, 5 p sep by 4 d, 8 d, turn. R, 3 d, 2 p sep by 3 d, 3 d, join to free p of 3 ring cluster of 11th row, 3 d, 2 p sep by 3 d, 3 d, cl r, turn. Ch, 8 d, 5 p sep by 4 d, 8 d, turn. Repeat from beginning all around, tie and cut.
13th Row—Repeat the 7th row.
14th Row—Repeat the 8th row.
15th Row—R, 7 d, join to center p of ch of 14th row, 7 d, cl r, turn. Ch, 8 d, p, 8 d, turn. Repeat from beginning all around, tie and cut.
16th Row—Repeat 9th row.
17th Row—Repeat the 10th row.

TUMBLER DOILY

Work center ring, 1st and 2nd rows same as plate doily.
Next Row—R, 2 d, 5 p sep by 2 d, 2 d, cl r, turn. Ch, 2 d, 2 p sep by 2 d, 2 d, join to 2nd p of 1st r of motif of 2nd row, 2 d, 2 p sep by 2 d, 2 d, turn. R, 2 d, 5 p sep by 2 d, 2 d, cl r, turn. Ch, 2 d, 2 p sep by 2 d, 2 d, join to 3rd free p of next r of same motif, 2 d, 2 p sep by 2 d, 2 d, turn. Complete edge in same manner same as 10th row of plate doily, tie and cut.

BREAD AND BUTTER PLATE

Work center ring, 1st, 2nd, 3rd and 4th rows of plate doily.
Next Row—R, 2 d, 5 p sep by 2 d, 2 d, cl r, turn. Ch, 2 d, 2 p sep by 2 d, 2 d, join to 5th p of ch of 4th row, 2 d, 2 p sep by 2 d, 2 d, turn. R, 2 d, 5 p sep by 2 d, 2 d, cl r, turn. Ch, 2 d, 2 p sep by 2 d, 2 d, join to 1st p of next ch of 4th row, 2 d, 2 p sep by 2 d, 2 d, turn. Continue edge in same manner as 10th row of plate doily, tie and cut.

Fairy Ring Doily

Materials Required—AMERICAN THREAD COMPANY "STAR" CROCHET COTTON, Size 30

5—150 Yd. Balls.
1 Tatting Shuttle and 1 ball are required for working.
Doily measures about 16 inches.

R, 18 long picots, tie and cut thread.

2nd Row. L R, 3 d, 7 p, 3 d, close r, * turn, ¼ inch space. S R, 3 d, join to p of r in previous row, 3 d, close r, turn, ¼ inch space. L R, 3 d, join to 7th p of last L R, 6 p, 3 d, close r. Repeat from * all around and join to 1st L R.

3rd Row. R, 3 d, p, 2 d, join to center p of L R in previous row, 2 d, p, 3 d, close r, turn, ¼ inch space. R, 3 d, 3 p sep by 3 d, 3 d, close r, * turn, ¼ inch space. R, 3 d, join to 3rd p of opposite r, 2 d, join to 3rd p of L R in previous row, 2 d, p, 3 d, close r, turn, ¼ inch space. L R, 3 d, join to 3d p of opposite r, 10 p, 3 d, close r, turn, space. R, 3 d, join to p of opposite r, 2 d, skip 1 p of same L R of last row, join to next p, 2 d, p, 3 d, close r, turn, space. R, 3 d, join to 11th p of last L R, 3 d, 2 p sep by 3 d, 3 d, close r, turn, space. R, 3 d, join to 3rd p of opposite r, 2 d, join to 3rd p of L R in previous row, 2 d, p, 3 d, close r, turn, space. L R, 3 d, join to 3rd p of opposite r, 10 p, 3 d, close r, turn, space. R, 3 d, join to 3rd p of opposite r, 2 d, skip 1 p of same L R in previous row, join to next p, 2 d, p, 3 d, close r, turn, space. R, 3 d, join to 11th p of last L R, 3 d, 2 p sep by 3 d, 3 d, close r, turn, space. R, 3 d, join to 3rd p of opposite r, 2 d, join to center p of L R in previous row, 2 d, p, 3 d, close r, turn, space. L R, 3 d, join to 3rd p of opposite r, 10 p, 3 d, close r, turn, repeat from * all around, tie and cut thread.

4th Row. R, 3 d, 3 p sep by 3 d, 3 d, close r, turn, space. R, 3 d, p, * 3 d, join to center p of r in previous row, 3 d, p, 3 d, close r, (turn, space. R, 3 d, join to 3rd p of opposite r, 3 d, 2 p sep by 3 d, 3 d, close r, turn, space. R, 3 d, join to 3rd p of opposite r, 3 d, 2 p sep by 3 d, 3 d, close r) 2 times, turn, space. R, 3 d, join to 3rd p of opposite r, 3 d, 2 p sep by 3 d, 3 d, close r, turn, space. R, 3 d, join to 3rd p of opposite r, repeat from * all around and join.

5th and 6th Rows. Join thread to p of last row. * Ch, 4 d, p, 4 d, join to next p of previous row, repeat from * all around, join and cut thread.

7th Row. Small Motif. * R, 4 d, p, 4 d, join to p of ch in previous row, 4 d, p, close r. (R, 4 d, join to 3rd p of last r, 4 d, 2 p sep by 4 d, 4 d, close r) 3 times, join 4th r to 1st r, tie and cut. Repeat from *, skip 1 p of last row, join next motif to next p and join 2nd p of 2nd r to p of last motif.

8th Row. * S R, 3 d, p, 3 d, close r, turn, space. R, 3 d, p, 3 d, join to p of previous row, 3 d, p, 3 d, close r, turn, space. S R, 3 d, join to p of last S R, 3 d, close r, turn, space. R, 3 d, join to 3rd p of opposite r, 3 d, 2 p sep by 3 d, 3 d, close r, turn, space. S R, 3 d, p, 3 d, close r, turn, space. R, 3 d, join to 3rd p of opposite r, 3 d, 2 p sep by 3 d, 3 d, close r, turn, space, repeat from * all around, tie and cut thread.

9th Row. Work same as 8th row, join 1 S R to p of 2 S R and 2 S R with the 1 S R.

10th Row. R, 3 d, 3 p sep by 3 d, 3 d, close r, turn, space. R, 3 d, p, 3 d, join to p of last row, 3 d, p, 3 d, close r, turn, space. * L R, 3 d, join to 3rd p of opposite r, 8 p, 3 d, close r, turn, space. R, 3 d, join to opposite r, 3 d, join to p of last row, 3 d, p, 3 d, close r, turn, space. R, 3 d, join to 9th p of L R, 3 d, 2 p sep by 3 d, 3 d, close r, turn, space. R, 3 d, join to p of opposite r, 3 d, join to p of last row, 3 d, p, 3 d, close r, repeat from * all around, tie and cut thread.

11th Row. Same as 7th row, join small motifs to center p of L R in last row.

Work large motif around edge as follows. **1st Row.** R, 12 p, close r, tie and cut thread.

2nd Row. L R, 3 d, 7 p, 3 d, close r, * turn, space. S R, 3 d, join to center r, 3 d, close r, turn, space. L R, 3 d, join to 7th p of last L R, 6 p, 3 d, close r, repeat from * all around, tie and cut thread.

3rd Row. L R, 3 d, 5 p, join to p of small motif in last row, 5 p, 3 d, close r, turn, space. R, 3 d, p, 3 d, * join to 3rd p of L R in last row, 3 d, p, 3 d, close r, turn, space. R, 3 d, join to 11th p of last L R, 3 d, 2 p sep by 3 d, 3 d, close r, turn, space. R, 3 d, join to p of opposite r, 3 d, join to 5th p of same L R in last row, 3 d, p, 3 d, close r, turn, space. L R, 3 d, join to p of opposite r, 4 p, join to p of next small motif, 5 p, 3 d, close r, turn, space. R, 3 d, join to p of opposite r, 3 d, join to 3rd p of L R in last row, 3 d, p, 3 d, close r, turn, space. R, 3 d, join to 11th p of last r, 3 d, 2 p sep by 3 d, 3 d, close r, turn, space. R, 3 d, join to 3rd p of opposite r, 3 d, join to 5th p of same L R of last row, 3 d, p, 3 d, close r, turn, space. L R, 3 d, join to 3rd p of opposite r, 4 p, join to p of next small motif, 5 p, 3 d, close r, turn, space. R, 3 d, join to p of opposite r, 3 d, join to 3rd p of L R in last row, 3 d, p, 3 d, close r, turn, space. R, 3 d, join to 11th p of last L R, 3 d, 2 p sep by 3 d, close r, turn, space. R, 3 d, join to p of opposite r, 3 d, join to 5th p of same L R in last row, 3 d, p, 3 d, close r, repeat from *, tie and cut thread.

Work other motifs to correspond joining them together by center p of 2 L R.

Work a L R and join between the large motif on both sides of the motif as follows: R, 4 d, join to p of S R, 9 p, join to p of S R of next motif, 4 d, close r, tie and cut thread.

Nosegays

EDGING FOR INFANT'S DRESS

Materials Required—AMERICAN THREAD COMPANY "STAR" MERCERIZED TATTING COTTON

1—75 Yd. Ball will make about 3½ Yds. of Lace.

1 Shuttle.

R, 2 d, 7 p sep by 1 d, 2 d, cl r leaving about ⅛ inch space. ⅛ inch thread. R, 2 d, join to last p of previous r, 1 d, 6 p sep by 1 d, 2 d, cl r leaving about ⅛ inch space. ⅛ inch thread and continue rings for desired length.

BABY CAP

6 Months to 1 Year

Materials Required—AMERICAN THREAD COMPANY "STAR" MERCERIZED TATTING COTTON

4—75 Yd. Balls White or Colors.

1 Ball and 1 Shuttle.

Center Medallion. R, 1 d, 8 p sep by 2 d, 1 d, close r, tie and cut.

2nd Row. R, 3 d, join to a p of small ring just made, 3 d, close r, turn. Ch, 6 d, 3 p sep by 3 d, 6 d, turn. * R, 3 d, join to the next p of small ring, 3 d, close r, turn. Ch, 6 d, 3 p sep by 3 d, 6 d, turn, repeat from * all around, join, tie and cut.

3rd Row. * R, 3 d, join to center p of ch in 2nd row, 3 d, close r, turn. Ch, 9 d, 3 p sep by 3 d, 9 d, turn. R, 3 d, join to 1st p of next ch, 3 d, close r, turn. Ch, 9 d, 3 p sep by 3 d, 9 d, turn. R, 3 d, join to 3rd p of same ch, 3 d, close r, turn. Ch, 9 d, 3 p sep by 3 d, 9 d, turn and repeat from * all around, tie and cut.

Small Motif around Center Medallion. * Center and 1 row are worked the same as the center medallion joining the last 2 chs as follows: ch, 6 d, p, 3 d, join to center p of ch in last row, 3 d, p, 6 d, turn. R, 3 d, join to next p, 3 d, close r, turn. Ch, 6 d, p, 3 d, join to center p of next ch of last row, 3 d, p, 6 d, tie and cut.

2nd Motif is made in the same manner until you have 6 chs, the 7th ch is joined to the next free ch of 1st motif, the 8th ch is joined to the next ch of last row. Tie and cut.

3rd Motif is made the same as the 2nd motif joining to the 2nd ch instead of 1st, leaving 1 ch free between joinings and the center medallion. Repeat from * joining all 9 motifs in same manner.

3rd Row. R, 1 d, 9 p sep by 1 d, 1 d, cl r, turn. Ch, 7 d, p, 7 d, join to center p of ch in last row, 7 d, p, 7 d, turn. * R, 1 d, 4 p sep by 1 d, 1 d, join to center p of last r, 1 d, 4 p sep by 1 d, 1 d, cl r, turn. Ch, 7 d, turn. R, 1 d, 9 p sep by 1 d, 1 d, cl r, turn. Ch, 7 d, turn. R, 1 d, 9 p sep by 1 d, 1 d, cl r, turn. Ch, 7 d, join to p of opposite ch, 7 d, join to center p of next ch in 2nd row, 7 d, p, 7 d, repeat from *, join, tie and cut.

4th Row. R, 1 d, 9 p sep by 1 d, 1 d, close r, turn. Ch, 9 d, p, 9 d, p, 9 d, p, 9 d, turn. * R, 1 d, 4 p sep by 1 d, join to center p of last r, 1 d, 4 p sep by 1 d, 1 d, cl r, turn. Ch, 9 d, turn. R, 1 d, 4 p sep by 1 d, 1 d, join to center p in 3rd row, 1 d, 4 p sep by 1 d, 1 d, cl r, turn. Ch, 9 d, turn. R, 1 d, 9 p sep by 1 d, 1 d, close r, turn. Ch, 9 d, join to p of opposite ch, 9 d, p, 9 d, p, 9 d, repeat from * all around, tie and cut.

5th Row. R, 4 d, p, 4 d, join to p of ch in last row, 4 d, p, 4 d, cl r, turn. ⅛ inch thread. R, 4 d, 3 p sep by 4 d, 4 d, cl r, turn. ⅛ inch thread. R, 4 d, join to last p of 1st r, 4 d, p, 4 d, p, 4 d, cl r, turn. ⅛ inch thread. R, 4 d, join to last p of 2nd r, 4 d, p, 4 d, p, 4 d, cl r, turn,

⅛ inch thread, repeat from beginning leaving 4 chs free for back of neck.

6th Row. R, 2 d, 11 p sep by 2 d, 2 d, cl r, turn. Ch, 6 d, p, 2 d, p, 2 d, p, 6 d, turn. * R, 4 d, join to 2nd p of large r just made, 4 d, cl r, turn. Ch, 6 d, p, 2 d, join to p of 3rd r in 5th row, 2 d, p, 6 d, turn. R, 4 d, join to 4th p of 1st r made, 4 d, cl r, turn. Ch, 6 d, p 2 d, p, 2 d, p, 6 d, join to 6th p of 1st r made, 6 d, turn. R, 4 d, p, 4 d, cl r, turn. Ch, 6 d, turn. R, 2 d, 11 p sep by 2 d, 2 d, cl r, turn. Ch, 6 d, join to p of opposite ch, 2 d, p, 2 d, p, 6 d, turn. Repeat from * across row skipping 2 rings of 6th row between joinings and ending row with the ch after the 2nd small r. Without breaking thread start 7th row.

7th Row. Ch, 6 d, p, 2 d, p, 2 d, p, 6 d, turn. R, 2 d, 11 p sep by 2 d, 2 d, cl r, turn. Ch, 6 d, p, 2 d, p, 2 d, p, 6 d, turn. * R, 4 d, join to 2nd p of large r, 4 d, cl r, turn. Ch, 6 d, p, 2 d, p, 2 d, p, 6 d, turn. R, 4 d, join to 4th p of large r, 4 d, cl r, turn. Ch, 6 d, p, 2 d, p, 2 d, p, 6 d, join to 6th p of large r, 4 d, join to p of small r in 6th row, 6 d, turn. R, 2 d, 11 p sep by 2 d, 2 d, cl r, turn. Ch, 6 d, join to 1st p of opposite ch, 2 d, p, 2 d, p, 6 d, turn. Repeat from * across row, working a ch at end of row to correspond, tie and cut.

8th Row. R, 4 d, p, 4 d, join to center p of ch in 7th row, 4 d, p, 4 d, cl r, turn. ⅛ inch thread. R, 4 d, p, 4 d, p, 4 d, p, 4 d, cl r, turn. ⅛ inch thread. R, 4 d, join to 3rd p of 1st r, 4 d, p, 4 d, p, 4 d, cl r, turn. ⅛ inch thread. R, 4 d, join to 3rd p of 2nd r, 4 d, p, 4 d, p, 4 d, cl r, turn. ⅛ inch thread. R, 4 d, join to last p of 3rd r, 4 d, p, 4 d, p, 4 d, cl r, turn. ⅛ inch thread. R, 4 d, join to last p of 4th r, 4 d, p, 4 d, p, 4 d, cl r, turn. ⅛ inch thread. Repeat from beginning across row.

9th Row. Work same as 3rd row working 9 d in ch instead of 7 d and joining chs to every other r of 8th row.

10th Row. Starting at front of cap. R, 4 d, p, 4 d, join to p of center r of last row, 4 d, p, 4 d, cl r, turn. ⅛ inch thread. R, 4 d, p, 4 d, cl r, turn. ⅛ inch thread. R, 4 d, join to last p of last r, 4 d, p, 4 d, p, 4 d, cl r, turn. ⅛ inch thread. * R, 4 d, join to last p of last r, 4 d, join to center p of next center r of last row, 4 d, p, 4 d, cl r, turn. ⅛ inch thread. R, 4 d, join to p of last small r, 4 d, cl r, turn. ⅛ inch thread. R, 4 d, join to p of last large r, 4 d, p, 4 d, p, 4 d, cl r, turn. ⅛ inch thread. Repeat from * across front of cap and continue across back of cap shaping to fit.

EDGING FOR BIB

Materials Required—AMERICAN THREAD COMPANY "STAR" MERCERIZED TATTING COTTON

1—75 Yd. Ball White or Colors.

To make bib, cut a piece of material 7 x 7 inches. Fold through the center and place a marker 1¾ inches from double edge and round all corners to shape bib. Hollow out the neck to fit. Face the bib with some soft material and bind edges with a bias tape allowing about 10 inches for ties.

Tatted Edge. Use 1 Shuttle and 1 Ball.

R, 5 d, 7 p sep by 2 d, 5 d, cl r. * R, 5 d, join to last p of last r, 2 d, 4 p sep by 2 d, 5 d, cl r, turn. Ch, 5 d, 5 p sep by 2 d, 5 d, turn. R, 5 d, join to 2nd p of last r, 6 p sep by 2 d, 5 d, cl r and repeat from * for desired length. Sew to bib at picots as illustrated.

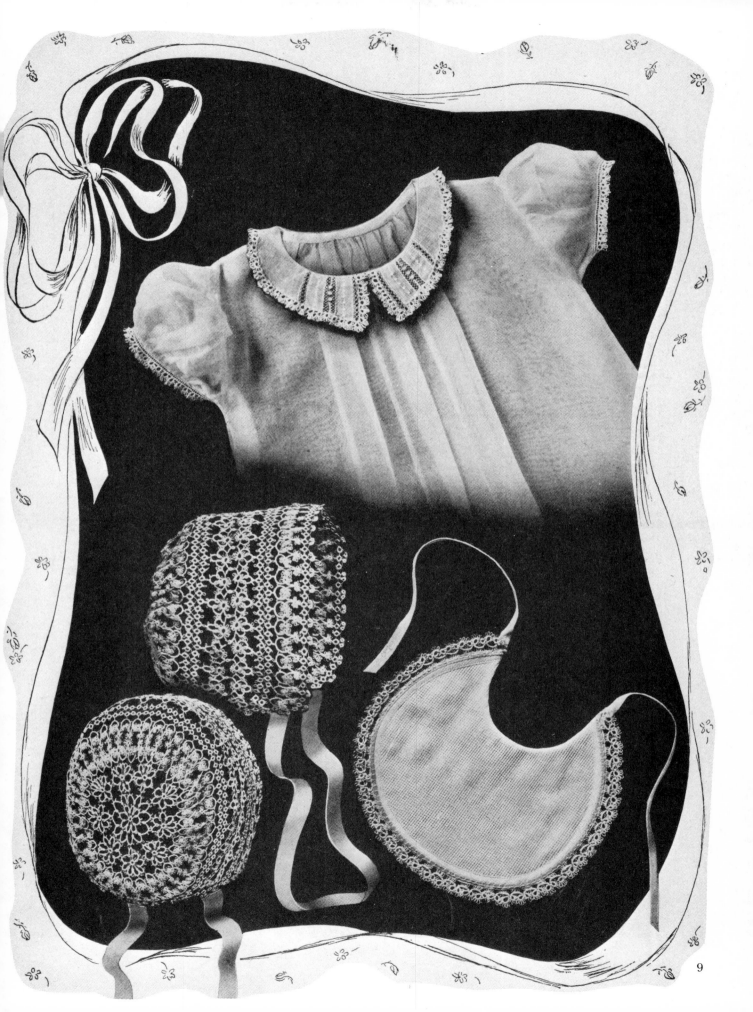

Frosted Star

MATERIALS: J. & P. Coats or Clark's O.N.T. Best Six Cord Mercerized Crochet, *Size 20, 2 balls of White.*

Doily measures 15 inches from point to point.

Tie ball and shuttle threads together. **CENTER MOTIF . . . 1st rnd:** R of 5 ds, 2 sm p's sep by 6 ds, 4 ds, p, 4 ds, 2 sm p's sep by 6 ds, 5 ds, cl. Tie. (R of 5 ds, join to first sm p of previous r, 6 ds, sm p, 4 ds, p, 4 ds, 2 sm p's sep by 6 ds, 5 ds, cl. Tie) 5 times, joining last r to first r as previous r's were joined. Tie and cut. **2nd rnd:** Attach thread to 2nd sm p of first r. * Ch of 8 ds, p, 8 ds, join to next sm p of same r. Ch of 4 ds, p, 4 ds, join to 2nd sm p of next r. Repeat from * around. Tie and cut. **3rd rnd:** R of 10 ds, join to p of sm ch of preceding rnd, * 10 ds, cl. Rw, ch of 4 ds, 4 p's sep by 4 ds, 4 ds. Join to p of next ch. Ch of 4 ds, 4 p's sep by 4 ds, 4 ds. Rw, r of 10 ds, join to p of next sm ch. Repeat from * around. Tie and cut. **4th rnd:** R of 10 ds, join to 3rd p of first ch of preceding rnd, * 10 ds, cl. Rw, ch of 4 ds,

3 p's sep by 4 ds, 4 ds. Rw, r of 10 ds, skip 2 p's, join to 2nd p of next ch, 10 ds, cl. Rw, ch of 4 ds, 9 p's sep by 4 ds, 4 ds. Rw, r of 10 ds, skip 4 p's, join to next p. Repeat from * around. Tie and cut.

FLOWER (Make 12) . . . R of 5 ds, 3 sm p's sep by 8 ds, 5 ds, cl. Tie. (R of 5 ds, join to first sm p of previous r, 8 ds, 2 sm p's sep by 8 ds, 5 ds, cl) 5 times, joining last r to sm p of first r. Tie and cut. **5th rnd:** Attach thread to free p of any r of first flower and make a ch of 4 ds, 3 p's sep by 4 ds, 4 ds, join to p of next r of same flower. Ch of 4 ds, p, 4 ds, join to center p of sm ch of preceding rnd of doily, * 4 ds, p, 4 ds, join to p of next r of flower. Ch of 4 ds, 3 p's sep by 4 ds, 4 ds, join to p of next r. Reversing curve of chain, ch of 5 ds, 4 p's sep by 5 ds, 5 ds. Rw, r of 10 ds, join to center p of next-to-last ch, 10 ds, cl. Rw, ch of 5 ds, p, 5 ds. Rw, r of 10 ds, join to 3rd p of large ch of doily, 10 ds, cl. Rw, ch of 5 ds, p, 5 ds. Rw, r of 10 ds, join to 7th p of same ch, 10 ds, cl. Rw, ch of 5 ds, p, 5 ds. Rw, r of 10 ds, p, 10 ds, cl. Rw, ch of 5 ds, 4 p's sep by 5 ds, 5 ds, join to free p

of any r of next flower. Reversing curve of chain, make ch of 4 ds, p, 4 ds, join to p of previous r, 4 ds, p, 4 ds, join to p of next r of 2nd flower. Ch of 4 ds, p, 4 ds, join to center p of next sm ch of doily. Repeat from * around. Join to first ch. Tie and cut.

6th rnd: Attach thread to p of any r of unattached flower, ch of 4 ds, p, 4 ds, join to 3rd p of 4-p ch of doily, 4 ds, p, 4 ds, join to p of next r of same flower, ch of 4 ds, 3 p's sep by 4 ds, 4 ds, join to p of next r of flower, ch of 4 ds, p, 4 ds, join to 2nd p of next 4-p ch of doily, 4 ds, p, 4 ds, join to p of next r of flower, (ch of 4 ds, 3 p's sep by 4 ds, 4 ds, join to p of next r of same flower) 3 times. Join to first ch of same flower. Reversing curve of chain, ch of 4 ds, 4 p's sep by 4 ds, 4 ds. * Rw, r of 10 ds, skip next ch, join to first p of next ch of flower, 10 ds, cl. Rw, ch of 4 ds, 3 p's sep by 4 ds, 4 ds. Rw, r of 10 ds, join to same p as last r, 10 ds, cl. Rw, ch of 4 ds, 3 p's sep by 4 ds, 4 ds. Rw, r of 10 ds, join to 3rd p of same ch of flower, 10 ds, cl. Rw, ch of 4 ds, 3 p's sep by 4 ds, 4 ds. Rw, r of 10 ds, join to same p, 10 ds, cl. Rw, ch of 4 ds, 4 p's sep by 4 ds, 4 ds, join between chains of flower to correspond.

Continued on page 11.

Frosted Star

Continued from page 10.

Ch of 4 ds, join to last p of preceding ch, 4 ds, 2 p's sep by 4 ds, 4 ds. Rw, r of 10 ds, join to next free p of next ch, 10 ds, cl. Rw, ch of 4 ds, 3 p's sep by 4 ds, 4 ds, join to first ch of next flower. Reversing curve of chain, ch of 4 ds, join to last p of preceding ch, 4 ds, 2 p's sep by 4 ds, 4 ds, join to p of next r of same flower. (Ch of 4 ds, 3 p's sep by 4 ds, 4 ds, join to p of next r of same flower) twice. Ch of 4 ds, join to last p of preceding ch, 4 ds, 2 p's sep by 4 ds, 4 ds. Rw, r of 10 ds, join to 2nd p of adjoining 4-p ch of doily, 10 ds, cl. Rw, ch of 4 ds, 3 p's sep by 4 ds, 4 ds, join to p of any r of next unattached flower. Reversing curve of chain, ch of 4 ds, join to p of previous ch, 4 ds, 3 p's sep by 4 ds, 4 ds. Repeat from * around. Tie and cut.

7th rnd: * R of 10 ds, join to center p of free ch of any flower along side of doily, 10 ds, cl. Rw, ch of 4 ds, 3 p's sep by 4 ds, 4 ds. R of 10 ds, join to same p, 10 ds, cl. Rw, ch as before. Rw, lr of 15 ds, skip next 2 ch and r, join to first p of next ch, 15 ds, cl. Rw, ch as before. Rw, r of 10 ds, join to 2nd free p of next ch, 10 ds, cl. Rw, ch as before. Rw, r of 10 ds, join to center p of next ch (between 2 rings), 10 ds, cl. Rw, ch as before. Rw, r of 10 ds, join to same p, 10 ds, cl. Rw, ch as before. Rw, r of 4 ds, 3 p's sep by 4 ds, 4 ds, cl. Rw, ch of 4 ds, 5 p's sep by 4 ds. Rw, r of 4 ds, p, 4 ds, join to center p of preceding r, 4 ds, p, 4 ds, cl. Rw, ch of 4 ds, 3 p's sep by 4 ds, 4 ds. Rw, r of 10 ds, skip next ch of doily, join to center p of next ch (between 2 rings), 10 ds, cl. Rw, ch as before. Rw, r of 10 ds, join to same p, 10 ds, cl. Rw, ch as before. Rw, r of 10 ds, join to same p, 10 ds, cl. Rw, ch as before. Rw, r of 10 ds, join to 2nd p of next ch of doily, 10 ds, cl. Rw, ch as before. Rw, lr of 15 ds, join to last p of next ch, 15 ds, cl. Rw, ch as before. Repeat from * around. Tie and cut.

Filigree Scroll

(at the left in the photo above)

MATERIALS: J. & P. Coats or Clark's O.N.T. Best Six Cord Mercerized Crochet, *Size 30, 1 ball of White.*

Doily measures 4 inches square.

1st rnd: R of 2 ds, 4 p's sep by 2 ds, 3 ds, 3 p's sep by 4 ds, 3 ds, 4 p's sep by 2 ds, 2 ds, cl. (Rw, ch of 3 ds, 11 p's sep by 2 ds. Rw, r of 2 ds, 4 p's sep by 2 ds, 3 ds, join to 5th p of preceding r, 4 ds, join to center p of preceding r, 4 ds, p, 3 ds, 4 p's sep by 2 ds, 2 ds, cl) 3 times, joining last r to p of first r and last ch to base of first r. Tie and cut. **2nd rnd:** R of 14 ds, join to 3rd p of ch of preceding rnd, 14 ds, cl. Rw, ch of 3 ds, sm p, * 7 ds, p, 15 ds. Sp of ⅛ inch. R of 3 ds (catch in the thread to hold chain in place), sm p, 10 ds, p, 10 ds, sm p, 3 ds, cl. (R of 3 ds, join to sm p of previous r, 10 ds, p, 10 ds, sm p, 3 ds, cl) 4 times. R of 3 ds, join to sm p of previous r, 10 ds, p, 10 ds, join to free sm p of first r (flower made). With wrong side of work toward you, carry threads over to opposite sm p and fasten. Ch of 15 ds, p, 7 ds, sm p, 3 ds. Rw, r of 14 ds, join to 9th p of same ch, 14 ds, cl. R of 14 ds, join to 3rd p of next ch, 14 ds, cl. Rw, ch of 3 ds, join to sm p of previous ch. Repeat from * around. Tie and cut. **3rd rnd:** R of 14 ds, join to p of first ch of preceding rnd, 14 ds, cl. * Rw, r of 14 ds, p, 14 ds, cl. Rw, ch of 14 ds, join to p of first r of flower, ch of 14 ds. Rw, r of 14 ds, join to p of previous r, 14 ds, cl. R of 14 ds, join to p of 2nd r of flower, 14 ds, cl. Reversing curve of ch, ch of 3 ds, 21 p's sep by 2 ds, 3 ds. Rw, r of 14 ds, join to p of 3rd r of flower, 14 ds, cl. R of 14 ds, p, 14 ds, cl. Reversing curve of ch, make a ch of 14 ds, join to p of 4th r of flower, 14 ds. Rw, r of 14 ds, join to p of previous r, 14 ds, cl. Rw, r of 14 ds, join to p of next ch, 14 ds, cl. Reversing curve of ch, ch of 3 ds, 11 p's sep by 2 ds, 3 ds. Rw, r of 14 ds, join to p of next ch, 14 ds, cl. Repeat from * around. Tie and cut.

Maypole Dance

(at the right in the photo)

MATERIALS: J. & P. Coats Tatting-Crochet, *Size 70, 3 balls . . . Linen, 3 x 18 inches (for 6 coasters).*

Starting at flower motif in the outside row, r of 3 ds, p, (4 ds, p) twice; 3 ds, cl. Rw, ch of (5 ds, p) twice; 5 ds. * Rw, r of 3 ds, p, 4 ds, join to 2nd p of first r, 4 ds, p, 3 ds, cl. Rw, ch of (5 ds, p) twice; 5 ds. Repeat from * 2 more times. Fasten at base of first r. This completes a flower. Ch of 9 ds, p, 3 ds. Rw, sm r of 9 ds, p, 5 ds, p, 4 ds, cl. Rw, sm r of 3 ds, join to p in preceding ch, 6 ds, p, 3 ds, p, 6 ds, cl. Rw, ch of 10 ds. Rw, lr of 12 ds, p, 12 ds, cl. Ch of 10 ds. Rw, sm r of 6 ds, p, 3 ds, p, 6 ds, p, 3 ds, cl. Rw, sm r of 4 ds, join to last p of first sm r, 5 ds, p, 9 ds, cl. Ch of 3 ds, join to last p of the other sm r, 9 ds. R of 3 ds, p, (4 ds, p) twice; 3 ds, cl. Rw, ch of 5 ds, p, 5 ds, join to first p of last ch of corresponding flower motif, 5 ds. Rw, and complete flower as before. Fasten at base of first r of flower.

Make 2 more groups same as this, but joining them to the preceding groups at the 2 p's of sm r's and at the p of lr. These 3 groups make a half circle. Make another half circle in this manner.

Cut 6 circles of linen, each 3 inches in diameter. Make a narrow hem around each piece and sew lace to linen along the edges.

Pretty Petal Doily

This Doily may be made with any of the AMERICAN THREAD COMPANY products listed below.

Material	Quantity	Approx. diameter of Doily
"STAR" Tatting Cotton, Article 25, or	5 balls White or Colors	8 inches
"STAR" Mercerized Crochet Cotton, Article 20, Size 30, or	1 ball White or Color	10 inches
"GEM" Mercerized Crochet Cotton, Article 35, Size 30	1 ball White or Color	10 inches

1 Shuttle and 1 Ball.

CENTER MEDALLION—R, 1 d, 8 p sep by 3 d, 2 d, cl r, tie and cut.

1st Row—R, 4 d, p, 4 d, join to p of center r, 4 d, p, 4 d, cl r, turn. * Ch, 5 d, 5 p sep by 3 d, 5 d, turn. R, 4 d, join to last p of last r made, 4 d, join to next p of center r, 4 d, p, 4 d, cl r, turn. Repeat from * 6 times joining last r to 1st r. Ch, 5 d, 5 p sep by 3 d, 5 d, tie and cut.

2nd Row—* R, 5 d, p, 5 d, join to 2nd p of ch of 1st row, 5 d, p, 5 d, cl r, turn. Ch, 5 d, 5 p sep by 3 d, 5 d, turn. R, 5 d, p, 5 d, join to 4th p of same ch of 1st row, 5 d, p, 5 d, cl r, turn. Ch, 5 d, 5 p sep by 3 d, 5 d, turn. Repeat from * 7 times, tie and cut.

3rd Row—R, 5 d, p, 5 d, join to center p of ch of 2nd row, 5 d, p, 5 d, cl r, turn. Ch, 5 d, 5 p sep by 4 d, 5 d, turn. * R, 5 d, p, 5 d, join to center p of next ch of 2nd row, 5 d, p, 5 d, cl r, turn. Ch, 5 d, 5 p sep by 4 d, 5 d, turn. Repeat from * all around, tie and cut.

EDGE MEDALLION: CLOVERLEAF—* R, 8 d, 5 p sep by 3 d. 8 d, cl r. Repeat from * twice, tie and cut.

CENTER RING—R, 1 d, 8 p sep by 3 d, 2 d, cl r, tie and cut.

1st Row—R, 4 d, p, 4 d, join to p of center r, 4 d, p, 4 d, cl r, turn. Ch, 5 d, 3 p sep by 3 d, 3 d, join to 2nd p of one r of cloverleaf, 3 d, p, 5 d, turn. R, 4 d, join to last p of last r made, 4 d, join to next p of center r, 4 d, p, 4 d, cl r, turn. Ch, 5 d, p, 3 d, join to 4th p of last r of cloverleaf, 3 d, 3 p sep by 3 d, 5 d, turn. * R, 4 d, join to last p of last r made, 4 d, join to next p of center r, 4 d, p, 4 d, cl r, turn. Ch, 5 d, 5 p sep by 3 d, 5 d, turn. Repeat from * 5 times tie and cut.

2nd Row—R, 5 d, p, 5 d, join to 4th p of 1st r of cloverleaf, 5 d, p, 5 d, cl r, turn. Ch, 5 d, 5 p sep by 3 d, 5 d, turn. R, 5 d, p, 5 d, join to 2nd p of 2nd r of cloverleaf, 5 d, p, 5 d, cl r, turn. Ch, 5 d, 5 p sep by 3 d, 5 d, turn. R, 5 d, p, 5 d, join to 4th p of same r of cloverleaf, 5 d, p, 5 d, cl r, turn. Ch, 5 d, 5 p sep by 3 d, 5 d, turn. R, 5 d, p, 5 d, join to center free p of 3rd r of cloverleaf, 5 d, p, 5 d, cl r, turn. Ch, 5 d, 5 p sep by 3 d, 5 d, turn. R, 5 d, p, 5 d, join to center free p of same ch that the 3rd cloverleaf is joined, 5 d, p, 5 d, cl r, turn. Ch, 5 d, 5 p sep by 3 d, 5 d, turn. R, 5 d, p, 5 d, join to center p of next ch, 5 d, p, 5 d, cl r, turn. * Ch, 5 d, 5 p sep by 3 d, 5 d, turn. R, 5 d, p, 5 d, join to 2nd p of next ch, 5 d, p, 5 d, cl r, turn. Ch, 5 d, 5 p sep by 3 d, 5 d, turn. R, 5 d, p, 5 d, join to 4th p of same ch, 5 d, p, 5 d, cl r, turn. Repeat from * once. Ch, 5 d, 2 p sep by 3 d, 3 d, join to center p of ch of center Medallion, 3 d, p, 3 d, p, 5 d, turn. * R, 5 d, p, 5 d, join to 2nd p of next ch of 1st row, 5 d, p, 5 d, cl r, turn. Ch, 5 d, 5 p sep by 3 d, 5 d, turn. R, 5 d, p, 5 d, join to 4th p of same ch, 5 d, p, 5 d, cl r, turn. Ch, 5 d, 5 p sep by 3 d, 5 d, turn. R, 5 d, p, 5 d, join to center p of next ch of 1st row, 5 d, p, 5 d, cl r, turn. Ch, 5 d, 5 p sep by 3 d, 5 d, turn. R, 5 d, p, 5 d, join to center free p of next ch, 5 d, p, 5 d, cl r, turn. Ch, 5 d, 5 p sep by 3 d, 5 d, tie and cut.

Work a 2nd edge Medallion in same manner, skip one ch of center Medallion, join center p of 10th ch to center p of next ch of center Medallion and joining the center p of the 12th and 13th ch to the 8th and 7th ch of 1st edge Medallion. Work 6 more edge Medallions in same manner, joining last Medallion to 1st Medallion to correspond.

Snowflake Tablecloth

Materials Required: AMERICAN THREAD COMPANY "STAR" MERCERIZED CROCHET COTTON, Article 20, Size 10, 38 balls, Ecru, White or Cream, or
"GEM" MERCERIZED CROCHET COTTON, Article 35, Size 10, 29 balls.

For smaller Motifs and Cloth use Size 20 or 30.
Each Motif measures about 5¾ inches. 117 Motifs 9 x 13 are required for cloth measuring about 52 x 75 inches.
1 Shuttle and 1 Ball.

MOTIF—R, 1 d, 13 p sep by 2 d, 1 d, cl r, tie and cut.

2nd Row—R, 2 d, p, 2 d, join to any p of 1st r, 2 d, p, 2 d, cl r. ¼ inch space, turn. R, 5 d, 3 p sep by 5 d, 5 d, cl r. * ¼ inch space, turn. R, 2 d, join to 3rd p of small r, 2 d, join to next p of center r, 2 d, p, 2 d, cl r. ¼ inch space, turn. R, 5 d, join to 3rd p of corresponding r, 5 d, p, 5 d, p, 5 d, cl r. Repeat from * until you have 13 rings, join to correspond, tie and cut.

3rd Row—R, 4 d, join to p of r of 2nd row, 4 d, cl r, turn. Ch, 4 d, 3 p sep by 3 d, 4 d, turn. * R, 4 d, join to next p of next r of 2nd row, 4 d, cl r, turn. Ch, 4 d, 3 p sep by 3 d, 4 d, turn. Repeat from * all around, tie and cut.

4th Row—R, 5 d, join to 1st p of ch of 3rd row, 5 d, cl r, turn. ¼ inch space. R, 5 d, 3 p sep by 5 d, 5 d, cl r, * turn. ¼ inch space. R, 5 d, join to next p of same ch, 5 d, cl r, turn. ¼ inch space. R, 5 d, join to 3rd p of corresponding r, 5 d, p, 5 d, p, 5 d, cl r. Repeat from * once, turn. ¼ inch space. R, 5 d, join to 1st p of next ch, 5 d, cl r. Continue all around in the same manner, tie and cut.

5th Row—R, 5 d, p, 5 d, join to p of any r of 4th row, 5 d, p, 5 d, cl r, turn. Ch, 8 d, p, 4 d, p, 8 d, turn. R, 5 d, p, 5 d, join to p of next r of 4th row, 5 d, p, 5 d, cl r, turn. Ch, 8 d, p, 4 d, p, 8 d, turn. * R, 5 d, p, 5 d, skip one r of 4th row, join in p of next r, 5 d, p, 5 d, cl r, turn. Ch, 8 d, p, 4 d, p, 8 d, turn. Repeat from * all around, tie and cut.

2nd Motif—Repeat the 1st 4 rows of 1st motif.

Next Row—R, 5 d, p, 5 d, join to p of any r of 4th row, 5 d, p, 5 d, cl r, turn. Ch, 8 d, p, 4 d, p, 8 d, turn. R, 5 d, p, 5 d, join to p of next r of 4th row, 5 d, p, 5 d, cl r, turn. Ch, 8 d, p, 4 d, p, 8 d, turn. R, 5 d, p, 5 d, skip 1 r of 4th row, join to p of next r, 5 d, p, 5 d, cl r, turn. Repeat from * 3 times. Ch, 8 d, join to 1st p of ch of 1st motif, 4 d, join to next p of same ch, 8 d, turn. * R, 5 d, p, 5 d, skip 1 r of 2nd motif, join to p of next r, 5 d, p, 5 d, cl r, turn. Ch, 8 d, join to 1st p of next ch of 1st motif, 4 d, join to next p of same ch, 8 d, turn. Repeat from * once and finish motif same as 1st motif. Join 3rd motif to 2nd motif in same manner leaving 2 free chs for joining small motif. Join 4th motif to 3rd and 1st motif in same manner.

Joining Motif—R, 2 d, 8 p sep by 3 d, 1 d, cl r, tie and cut.

Next Row—R, 4 d, join to p of r, 4 d, cl r, turn. Ch, 8 d, join to 1st p of 1st free ch of 1st motif, 4 d, join to next p of same ch, 8 d, turn. R, 4 d, join to next p of center r, 4 d, cl r, turn. Ch, 8 d, join to 1st p of next free ch of same motif, 4 d, join to next p of same ch, 8 d, turn. R, 4 d, join to next p of center r, 4 d, cl r, turn. Ch, 8 d, join to 1st free p of ch of next motif, 4 d, join to next p of same ch, 8 d, turn and continue in same manner until all chs are joined, tie and cut.

Tatted Edgings

Tatted Edging No. 6611

Materials Required: AMERICAN THREAD COMPANY "STAR" TATTING COTTON, Article 25.

1 Shuttle and 1 Ball.

R, 3 d, 3 p sep by 3 d, 3 d, cl r, turn. Ch, 6 d, 5 p sep by 2 d, 6 d, turn. * R, 3 d, join to last p of last r made, 3 d, join to next p of same r, 3 d, p, 3 d, cl r, turn. Ch, 6 d, 5 p sep by 2 d, 6 d, turn. R, 3 d, join to last p of last r made, 3 d, join to next p of same r, 3 d, p, 3 d, cl r, turn. Ch, 6 d, 3 p sep by 2 d, 6 d. R, 3 d, 3 p sep by 3 d, 3 d, cl r, turn. Ch, 6 d, join to corresponding p of opposite ch, 2 d, 4 p sep by 2 d, 6 d, turn. Repeat from * for desired length. * R, 3 d, join to last p of last r made, 3 d, join to next p of same r, 3 d, p, 3 d, cl r, turn. Ch, 6 d, 5 p sep by 2 d, 6 d, turn. Repeat from * once. Working across lower edge R, 3 d, join to last p of last r made, 3 d, join to center p of same group, 3 d, join to next free p of same group, 3 d, cl r, turn. * Ch, 6 d, 5 p sep by 2 d, 6 d, join to center p of 3 p ch, 6 d, 5 p sep by 2 d, 6 d, turn. R, 3 d, join to last p of last r made of next group, 3 d, join to center p of same group, 3 d, join to next free p of same group, 3 d, cl r. Repeat from * across row, tie and cut.

Tatted Edging No. 6612

1 Shuttle and 1 Ball.

CENTER MOTIF—R, 4 d, 3 p sep by 4 d, 4 d, cl r, turn. * Ch, 6 d, 3 p sep by 3 d, 6 d, turn. R, 4 d, join to last p of last r made, 4 d, join to next p of same r, 4 d, p, 4 d, cl r, turn. Repeat from * twice, join 4th r to 1st r. Ch, 6 d, 3 p sep by 3 d, 6 d, tie and cut.

1st Row—R, 4 d, join to 3rd p of ch of center motif, 4 d, cl r, turn. * Ch, 6 d, 3 p sep by 3 d, 6 d, turn. R, 4 d, join to 1st p of next ch, 4 d, cl r, turn. Ch, 6 d, 3 p sep by 3 d, 6 d, turn. R, 4 d, join to 3rd p of same ch, 4 d, cl r, turn. Repeat from * once. Ch, 6 d, 3 p sep by 3 d, 6 d, turn. R, 4 d, join to 1st p of next ch, 4 d, cl r, tie and cut. Work a center motif same as 1st center motif.

1st Row—R, 4 d, join to 3rd p of ch of center motif, 4 d, cl r, turn. Ch, 6 d, join to corresponding p of ch of 1st motif, 3 d, join to next p of same ch, 3 d, p, 6 d, turn and complete motif same as 1st motif. Join all motifs in same manner, tie and cut.

Tatted Edging No. 6613

1 Shuttle and 1 Ball.

Rings are made in White.

Chains are made in Yellow or any Color desired.

R, 3 d, 8 large p sep by 4 d, 1 d, cl r, tie and cut.

R, 3 d, 3 p sep by 3 d, 3 d, cl r, turn. Ch, 4 d, p, 4 d, join to p of center large r, 4 d, p, 4 d, turn. * R, 3 d, 3 p sep by 3 d, 3 d, cl r, turn. Ch, 4 d, p, 4 d, join to next p of large r, 4 d, p, 4 d, turn. Repeat from * 3 times, turn. R, 3 d, 3 p sep by 3 d, 3 d, cl r, turn. Ch, 3 d, 7 p sep by 3 d, 3 d, turn. R, 3 d, join to 3rd p of last r made, 3 d, p, 3 d, join to 1st p of next r, 3 d, cl r, turn. * Ch, 3 d, 7 p sep by 3 d, 3 d, turn. R, 3 d, join to 3rd p of same r, 3 d, p, 3 d, join to 1st p of next r, 3 d, cl r, turn. Repeat from * 3 times. Ch, 3 d, 7 p sep by 3 d, 3 d, tie and cut.

2nd MOTIF JOINING—Work until the last 2 chains, 10th ch is joined with 5th and 6th p to corresponding picots of 7th ch of 1st motif and 2nd and 3rd p of next ch to corresponding picots of next ch of 1st motif.

Tatted Edging No. 6614

1 Shuttle and 1 Ball.

MOTIF—R, 3 d, 3 p sep by 3 d, 3 d, cl r, turn. Ch, 6 d, 3 p sep by 3 d, 6 d, turn. * R, 3 d, join to last p of last r made, 3 d, join to next p of same r, 3 d, p, 3 d, cl r, turn. Ch, 6 d, 3 p sep by 3 d, 6 d, turn. Repeat from * twice, joining last r to corresponding p of first r, tie and cut.

Work a 2nd motif joining 3rd p of ch to corresponding p of 1st motif and joining 1st p of next ch to corresponding p of 1st motif. Join all motifs in same manner for desired length. **EDGE**—R, 3 d, join to 3rd p of 1st free ch of 1st motif, 3 d, cl r, turn. Ch, 6 d, 3 p sep by 3 d, 6 d, turn. R, 3 d, join to 1st free p of next free ch of 1st motif, 3 d, cl r, turn. Ch, 6 d, 3 p sep by 3 d, 6 d, turn. R, 3 d, join to 3rd p of same ch, 3 d, cl r, turn. * Ch, 6 d, 3 p sep by 3 d, 6 d, turn. R, 3 d, join to 1st free p of next free ch of same motif, 3 d, cl r, turn. Ch, 6 d, 3 p sep by 3 d, 6 d, turn. R, 3 d, join to 2nd free p of next free ch of next motif, 3 d, cl r, turn. Repeat from * across row. Work other end in same manner.

Tatted Edging No. 6615

1 Shuttle and 1 Ball.

R, 8 d, p, 2 d, p, 8 d, cl r. Opposite R, 8 d, p, 2 d, p, 8 d, cl r. Ch, 8 d, p, 8 d, turn. R, 8 d, join to 2nd p of 1st r made, 2 d, p, 6 d, p, 2 d, cl r. R, 2 d, join to last p of last r, 6 d, p, 2 d, p, 4 d, p, 4 d, cl r, turn. * Ch, 11 d, turn. R, 2 d, join to last p of last r, 4 d, 3 p sep by 2 d, 4 d, p, 2 d, cl r. R, 2 d, join to last p of last r, 4 d, 3 p sep by 2 d, 4 d, p, 2 d, cl r. R, 2 d, join to last p of last r, 4 d, 3 p sep by 2 d, 4 d, p, 4 d, cl r, turn. Ch, 11 d, turn. R, 4 d, join to last p of last r, 4 d, p, 2 d, p, 6 d, p, 2 d, cl r. R, 2 d, join to last p of last r, 6 d, p, 2 d, p, 8 d, cl r, turn. Ch, 8 d, join to p of opposite ch, 8 d, turn. R, 8 d, join to last p of last r, 2 d, p, 8 d, cl r, turn. R, 8 d, join to p of opposite r, 2 d, p, 8 d, cl r. Ch, 8 d, 3 p sep by 3 d, 8 d, turn. R, 8 d, join to p of opposite r, 2 d, p, 8 d, cl r, turn. R, 8 d, join to p of opposite r, 2 d, p, 8 d, cl r. Ch, 8 d, p, 8 d, turn. R, 8 d, join to free p of next to last r made, 2 d, join to free p of 9th r made, 6 d, p, 2 d, cl r. This forms a 4 ring group. R, 2 d, join to last p of last r, 6 d, p, 2 d, p, 4 d, p, 4 d, cl r, turn. Repeat from * for length desired, tie and cut.

Tatted Edging No. 6616

1 Shuttle and 1 Ball.

All rings are made in Color desired. Chains are made in White. R, 5 d, 3 p sep by 5 d, 5 d, cl r. Ch, 5 d, turn. * R, 5 d, 3 p sep by 5 d, 5 d, cl r. Ch, 5 d, turn. R, 5 d, join to last p of 1st r, 5 d, 2 p sep by 5 d, 5 d, cl r. Ch, 5 d, p, 5 d, join to last p of 2nd r, 5 d, turn. R, 5 d, 3 p sep by 5 d, 5 d, cl r. Ch, 5 d, p, 5 d, join to p of opposite ch, 5 d, turn. R, 5 d, join to last p of corresponding r, 5 d, 2 p sep by 5 d, 5 d, cl r. Ch, 5 d, p, 5 d, join to p of opposite ch, 5 d, p, 5 d, join to last p of next r at lower edge, 5 d, turn. R, 5 d, 3 p sep by 5 d, 5 d, cl r. Continue increasing in same manner until there are 5 rings at scalloped edge, then decrease until a ch of 5 d remains. Repeat from * for desired length, tie and cut.

Tatted Edging No. 6617

1 Shuttle and 1 Ball.

All rings are made in White and all chains are made in Yellow.

R, 4 d, 3 p sep by 4 d, 4 d, cl r, turn. Ch, 4 d, 5 p sep by 4 d, 4 d, turn. R, 4 d, join to last p of r just made, 4 d, 2 p sep by 4 d, 4 d, cl r, turn. Ch, 4 d, 5 p sep by 4 d, 4 d, turn. R, 4 d, join to last p of last r made, 4 d, 2 p sep by 4 d, 4 d, cl r, turn. ** Ch, 4 d, 7 p sep by 4 d, 4 d, turn. R, 4 d, p, 4 d, join to center p of last r made, 4 d, p, 4 d, cl r, turn. Ch, 4 d, 5 p sep by 4 d, 4 d, turn. R, 4 d, join to last p of last r made, 4 d, join to corresponding p of opposite r, 4 d, p, 4 d, cl r, turn. Ch, 4 d, 5 p sep by 4 d, 4 d, turn. R, 4 d, join to last p of last r made, 4 d, join to corresponding p of opposite r, 4 d, p, 4 d, cl r, turn. Ch, 4 d, 7 p sep by 4 d, 4 d, turn. R, 4 d, 3 p sep by 4 d, 4 d, cl r, turn. * Ch, 4 d, 2 p sep by 4 d, 4 d, join to center p of opposite ch, 4 d, 2 p sep by 4 d, 4 d, turn. R, 4 d, join to last p of last r made, 4 d, 2 p sep by 4 d, 4 d, cl r, turn. Repeat from * once. Repeat from ** for desired length.

Materials required for the edgings on these two pages: AMERICAN THREAD COMPANY "STAR" TATTING COTTON, Article 25.

Tatted Edging No. 6622

1 Shuttle and 1 Ball.

R, 2 d, 9 p sep by 2 d, 2 d, cl r. * R, 2 d, join to last p of last r, 2 d, 8 p sep by 2 d, 2 d, cl r. R, 2 d, join to last p of last r made, 2 d, 8 p sep by 2 d, 2 d, cl r (clover), turn. Ch, 9 d, 6 p sep by 3 d, 9 d, turn. R, 2 d, 4 p sep by 2 d, 2 d, join to 5th p of last r made, 2 d, 4 p sep by 2 d, 2 d, cl r. Repeat from * for desired length of side. Corner. R, 2 d, join to last p of last r made, 2 d, 8 p sep by 2 d, 2 d, cl r. R, 2 d, join to last p of last r made, 2 d, 8 p sep by 2 d, 2 d, cl r, turn. Ch, 9 d, 3 p sep by 3 d, 9 d, turn. Work another clover, turn. Ch, 9 d, join to 3rd p of last ch, 3 d, join to 2nd p of same ch, 3 d, 9 d, turn. R, 2 d, 4 p sep by 2 d, 2 d, join to 5th p of last r made, 2 d, 4 p sep by 2 d, 2 d, cl r. Repeat from 1st * for side. Work all corners same as first corner.

More Tatted Edgings

Grand enough for wedding handkerchiefs—dainty enough for bassinettes: always beautiful.

Tatted Edging No. 6623

1 Shuttle.

R, 2 d, 9 p sep by 2 d, 2 d, cl r. R, 2 d, join to last p of last r, 2 d, 8 p sep by 2 d, 2 d, cl r. R, 2 d, join to last p of last r, 2 d, 8 p sep by 2 d, 2 d, cl r (clover), turn. Leave about 1/4 inch space. R, 2 d, p, 2 d, join to 7th p of last r made, 2 d, join to next p of same r, 2 d, 6 p sep by 2 d, 2 d, cl r. R, 2 d, join to last p of last r, 2 d, 8 p sep by 2 d, 2 d, cl r. R, 2 d, join to last p of last r, 2 d, 8 p sep by 2 d, 2 d, cl r, turn. 1/4 inch space. R, 2 d, p, 2 d, join to 7th p of last r made, 2 d, join to next p of same r, 2 d, p, 2 d, join to 5th p of the 3rd r of the 1st clover, 2 d, 4 p sep by 2 d, 2 d, cl r, complete clover, turn. 1/4 inch space. R, 2 d, p, 2 d, join to 7th p of last r made, 2 d, join to next p of same r, 2 d, p, 2 d, join to the 5th p of 3rd r of 2nd clover, 2 d, 4 p sep by 2 d, 2 d, cl r, complete clover. 1/4 inch space. R, 2 d, 4 p sep by 2 d, 2 d, join to 5th p of last r made, 2 d, 4 p sep by 2 d, 2 d, cl r, complete clover, turn. 1/4 inch space. R, 2 d, p, 2 d, join to 7th p of last r made, 2 d, join to next p of the same r, 2 d, p, 2 d, p, 2 d, join to 7th p of last r of 3rd clover, 2 d, join to next p of same r, 2 d, p, 2 d, p, 2 d, cl r. R, 2 d, join to last p of last r made, 2 d, p, 2 d, join to 7th p of 2nd r of 3rd clover, 2 d, join to next p of same r, 2 d, 5 p sep by 2 d, 2 d, cl r. R, 2 d, join to last p of last r made, 2 d, 8 p sep by 2 d, 2 d, cl r, turn. 1/4 inch space. R, 2 d, p, 2 d, join to 7th p of last r made, 2 d, join to the next p of same r, 2 d, p, 2 d, join to the 5th p of 3rd r of 5th clover, 2 d, 4 p sep by 2 d, 2 d, cl r, complete clover, turn. 1/4 inch space. R, 2 d, p, 2 d, join to 7th p of last r made, 2 d, join to next p of same r, 2 d, p, 2 d, join to 5th p of 3rd r of 6th clover, 2 d, 4 p sep by 2 d, 2 d, cl r, complete clover. Continue working in same manner as 2nd and 3rd clovers across row, working all corners same as 1st corner, tie and cut.

Tatted Edging No. 6624

1 Shuttle and 1 Ball.

CENTER RING—R, 3 d, 8 p sep by 5 d, 2 d, cl r, tie and cut.
MOTIF—R, 3 d, 3 p sep by 3 d, join to p of center r, 3 d, 3 p sep by 3 d, 3 d, cl r, turn. * Ch, 3 d, 7 p sep by 3 d, 3 d, turn. R, 3 d, p, 3 d, join to 2nd free p of last r made, 3 d, p, 3 d, join to next p of center r, 3 d, 3 p sep by 3 d, 3 d, cl r, turn. Repeat from * until there are 8 r's and 8 ch's, tie and cut.
Work a 2nd motif joining to 1st motif at center p of ch twice. Join a 3rd motif in same manner having 2 chains free on each side of motif. Join all motifs in same manner.
For a corner motif, join corner having 4 chains free on outside edge.
HEADING—R, 3 d, 7 p sep by 3 d, 3 d, cl r, turn. 3/8 inch space. R, 3 d, 7 p sep by 3 d, 3 d, cl r, turn. 3/8 inch space. R, 3 d, p, 3 d, join to 2nd p of 1st r made, 3 d, 5 p sep by 3 d, 3 d, cl r, turn. 3/8 inch space. R, 3 d, p, 3 d, join to 2nd p of corresponding r, 3 d, p, 3 d, join to center p of 1st free ch of motif to the left of corner, 3 d, 3 p sep by 3 d, 3 d, cl r, turn. 3/8 inch space. * R, 3 d, p, 3 d, join to 2nd p of

opposite r, 3 d, 5 p sep by 3 d, 3 d, cl r, turn. ⅜ inch space. Repeat from * twice. R, 3 d, p, 3 d, join to 2nd p of corresponding r, 3 d, p, 3 d, join to center p of next ch of same motif, 3 d, 3 p sep by 3 d, 3 d, cl r. R, 3 d, join to last p of last r made, 3 d, 7 p sep by 3 d, 3 d, cl r. R, 3 d, join to last p of last r made, 3 d, 2 p sep by 3 d, 3 d, join to center p of next free ch of 1st motif to right of corner motif, 3 d, 3 p sep by 3 d, 3 d, cl r, turn. ⅜ inch space. R, 3 d, p, 3 d, join to 2nd free p of corresponding r, 3 d, join to next p of same r, 3 d, 4 p sep by 3 d, 3 d, cl r, turn. ⅜ inch space. ** R, 3 d, p, 3 d, join to 2nd free picot of opposite r, 3 d, 5 p sep by 3 d, 3 d, cl r, turn. ⅜ inch space. R, 3 d, p, 3 d, join to corresponding p of opposite r, 3 d, 5 p sep by 3 d, 3 d, cl r, turn. ⅜ inch space. R, 3 d, p, 3 d, join to corresponding p of opposite ring, 3 d, join to center p of next ch of same motif, 3 d, 3 p sep by 3 d, 3 d, cl r, turn. ⅜ inch space. * R, 3 d, p, 3 d, join to corresponding p of opposite r, 3 d, 5 p sep by 3 d, 3 d, cl r, turn. ⅜ inch space. Repeat from * twice. R, 3 d, p, 3 d, join to corresponding p of opposite r, 3 d, join to center p of first free ch of next motif, 3 d, 3 p sep by 3 d, 3 d, cl r, turn. ⅜ inch space. R, 3 d, p, 3 d, join to corresponding p of opposite r, 3 d, 5 p sep by 3 d, 3 d, cl r, turn. ⅜ inch space. Repeat from ** to opposite corner and work corner same as first corner.

Tatted Edging No. 6625

1 Shuttle and 1 Ball.
R, 3 d, 7 p sep by 3 d, 3 d, cl r, turn. * Ch, 3 d, 7 p sep by 3 d, 3 d. R, 3 d, 5 p sep by 3 d, 3 d, cl r, turn. Ch, 3 d, 2 p sep by 3 d, 3 d, join to 2nd free p of large r, 3 d, 2 p sep by 3 d, 3 d, turn. R, 6 d, join to 2nd p of 5 p r, 6 d, cl r. R, 6 d, p, 6 d, cl r, turn. Ch, 3 d, 7 p sep by 3 d, 3 d, turn. R, 3 d, p, 3 d, join to p of last r made, 3 d, p, 3 d, join to center p of same 5 p r, 3 d, 5 p sep by 3 d, 3 d, cl r, turn. Ch, 3 d, 7 p sep by 3 d, 3 d, turn. R, 6 d, join to 2nd free p of last r made, 6 d, cl r. R, 6 d, p, 6 d, cl r, turn. Ch, 3 d, 5 p sep by 3 d, 3 d, turn. R, 3 d, p, 3 d, join to p of last small r made, 3 d, join to 2nd free p of large r, 3 d, 2 p sep by 3 d, 3 d, cl r. Ch, 3 d, 7 p sep by 3 d, 3 d, turn. R, 3 d, p, 3 d, join to center p of opposite ch, 3 d, 5 p sep by 3 d, 3 d, cl r, turn. Repeat from * for desired length.

Tatted Edging No. 6626

1 Shuttle and 1 Ball.
R, 6 d, p, 3 d, p, 3 d, cl r. R, 3 d, join to last p of last r made, 3 d, 3 p sep by 2 d, p, 3 d, cl r. R, 3 d, join to last p of last r made, 3 d, p, 6 d, cl r, turn. Ch, 3 d, p, 9 d, 3 p sep by 2 d, 9 d, p, 3 d, turn. * R, 6 d, join to last p of last r made, 3 d, p, 3 d, cl r, turn. Ch, 3 d, turn. R, 3 d, join to last p of last r made, 3 d, 3 p sep by 2 d, 3 d, p, 3 d, cl r, turn. Ch, 3 d, turn. R, 3 d, join to last p of last r made, 3 d, p, 6 d, cl r, turn. Ch, 3 d, join to corresponding p of opposite ch, 9 d, 3 p sep by 2 d, 9 d, p, 3 d, turn. R, 6 d, join to last p of last r made, 3 d, p, 3 d, cl r. R, 3 d, join to last p of last r, 3 d, p, 6 d, cl r. R, 3 d, join to last p of last r made, 3 d, 3 p sep by 2 d, 3 d, p, 3 d, cl r. R, 3 d, join to last p of last r, 3 d, p, 6 d, cl r, turn. Ch, 3 d, join to corresponding p of opposite ch, 9 d, 3 p sep by 2 d, 9 d, p, 3 d, turn. Repeat from * for length desired.

Tatted Edging No. 6627

1 Shuttle and 1 Ball.
Rings are made in Green.
Chains are made in White.
R, 3 d, 6 p sep by 2 d, 3 d, cl r, turn. * Ch, 3 d, 11 p sep by 2 d, 3 d. R, 3 d, 2 p sep by 2 d, 2 d, join to 3rd p of last r made, 2 d, 3 p sep by 2 d, 3 d, cl r, turn. Ch, 3 d, turn. R, 3 d, join to last p of last r made, 3 d, 7 p sep by 2 d, 3 d, p, 3 d, cl r, turn. Ch, 3 d, turn. R, 3 d, join to last p of last r made, 2 d, 5 p sep by 2 d, 3 d, cl r, turn. Repeat from * for desired length.

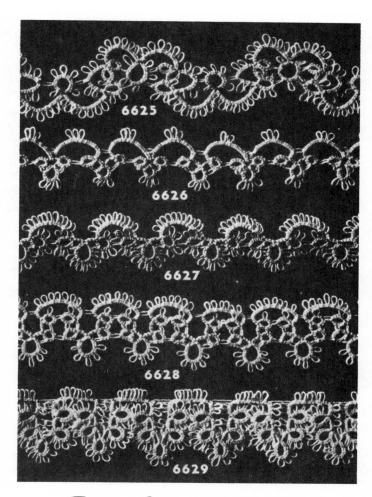

Tatted Edging No. 6628

1 Shuttle and 1 Ball.
R, 3 d, 3 p sep by 3 d, 3 d, cl r, turn. Ch, 3 d, 9 p sep by 3 d, 3 d, turn. R, 3 d, p, 3 d, join to center p of last r made, 3 d, p, 3 d, cl r, turn. Ch, 3 d, turn. R, 3 d, join to last p of last r made, 3 d, 2 p sep by 3 d, 3 d, cl r, turn. * Ch, 3 d, turn. R, 3 d, join to last p of last r made, 3 d, p, 3 d, cl r, turn. Ch, 3 d, turn. R, 3 d, join to last p of last r made, 3 d, 2 p sep by 3 d, 3 d, cl r, turn. Ch, 3 d, turn. R, 3 d, join to last p of last r made, 3 d, 2 p sep by 3 d, 3 d, cl r, turn. Ch, 3 d, join to last p of opposite ch, 3 d, 8 p sep by 3 d, 3 d, turn. R, 3 d, p, 3 d, join to center p of last r made, 3 d, p, 3 d, cl r, turn. Ch, 3 d, turn. R, 3 d, join to last p of last r made, 3 d, join to center p of opposite r, 3 d, p, 3 d, cl r, turn. Repeat from * for length desired.

Tatted Edging No. 6629

1 Shuttle and 1 Ball.
Ch, 3 d, large p, 2 d, 2 p sep by 2 d, 2 d, turn. R, 3 d, 7 p sep by 2 d, 3 d, cl r, turn. * Ch, 2 d, p, 2 d, turn. R, 3 d, join to last p of last r made, 2 d, 6 p sep by 2 d, 3 d, cl r, turn. Repeat from * 3 times. ** Ch, 2 d, 2 p sep by 2 d, 2 d, join to large p of opposite ch, 3 d, 7 p sep by 2 d, 3 d, large p, 2 d, 2 p sep by 2 d, 2 d, turn. R, 3 d, 2 p sep by 2 d, 2 d, join to center p of last r made, 2 d, 3 p sep by 2 d, 3 d, cl r, turn. Ch, 2 d, p, 2 d, turn. R, 3 d, join to last p of last r made, 2 d, p, 2 d, p, 2 d, join to center p of opposite r, 2 d, 3 p sep by 2 d, 3 d, cl r, turn. * Ch, 2 d, p, 2 d, turn. R, 3 d, join to last p of last r made, 2 d, 6 p sep by 2 d, 3 d, cl r, turn. Repeat from * twice. Repeat from ** for length desired.

Enchanted Doily

Materials Required—AMERICAN THREAD COMPANY "STAR" MERCERIZED CROCHET COTTON, Size 50

1—175 Yd. Ball.
1 Shuttle and 1 ball are used for making doily.
Doily measures about 7 inches.

1st Row. R, 3 d, p, 3 d, p, 3 d, p, 3 d, close r. Ch, 9 d. R, 3 d, p, 6 d, p, 3 d, close r. * Ch, 9 d. R, 3 d, join to 3rd p of 1st ring made, 3 d, p, 3d, p, 3 d, close r. Ch, 9 d. R, 3 d, p, 3 d, p, 3 d, p, 3 d, close r. Ch, 6 d, join to 3rd p of 2nd ring made, 6 d, p, 6 d. R, 3 d, join to last p of last r made, 3 d, join to center p of same ring, 3 d, p, 3 d, close r. Ch, 6 d, p, 6 d, p, 6 d. R, 3 d, join to last p of last ring made, 3 d, join to center p, 3 d, p, 3 d, close r. Ch, 6 d, p, 6 d, p, 6 d. R, 3 d, join to last p of last ring made, 3 d, join to center p, 3 d, join to 1st p of 1st ring of cluster, 3 d, close r. Ch, 9 d. R, 3 d, join to 3rd p of R, 3 d, p, 3 d, p, 3 d, close r. Ch, 9 d. R, 3 d, join to p of ch, 6 d, p, 3 d, close r. Repeat from *.

2nd Row. R, 3 d, p, 3 d, p, 3 d, p, 3 d, close r. Ch, 6 d. * R, 3 d, p, 3 d, p, 3 d, p, 3 d, close r. Ch, 6 d. R, 3 d, join to last p of 1st ring made, 3 d, join to center p, 3 d, p, 3 d, close r. Ch, 6 d, join to 2nd p of 1st row of ch 6 loop, 6 d, join to the 1st p of opposite ch 6 loop, 6 d. R, 3 d, join to 3rd p, 3 d, join to center p, 3 d, close r. Ch, 6 d. R, 3 d, join to 1st p of ch 6 of last row, 3 d, p, 3 d, p, 3 d, close r. Ch, 6 d. R, 3 d, join to last p of 2nd last ring made, 3 d, join to center p, join to 3rd p, 3 d, close r. Ch, 6 d, p, 6 d, p, 6 d. R, 3 d, join to 2nd last ring made, 3 d, join to 2nd p, 3 d, p, 3 d, close r. Ch, 6 d, p, 6 d, p, 6 d. R, 3 d, join to last p of last ring made, 3 d, join to center, 3 d, p, 3 d, close r. Ch, 6 d, p, 6 d, p, 6 d. R, 3 d, join to 2nd last ring made, 3 d, join to center, 3 d, join to 2nd p of ch 6 loop, 3 d, close r. Ch, 6 d. Repeat from *.

1st Section of 3rd Row. This is worked up and down, then joined.

R. 3 d, p, 3 d, p, 3 d, p, 3 d, close r. Ch, 6 d, p, 6 d, p, 6 d. R, 3 d, join to 3rd p of 1st r, 3 d, join to center p, 3 d, p, 3 d, close r. Ch, 6 d, p, 6 d, p, 6 d. R, 3 d, join to last r, 3 d, join to center, 3 d, p, 3 d, close r. Ch, 6 d, p, 6 d, p, 6 d. R, 3 d, join to last p of r, 3 d, join to center, 3 d, join to 1st p of 1st r, 3 d, close r. Ch, 6 d. R, 3 d, join to last p of ch, 3 d, p, 3 d, p, 3 d, close r. Ch, 6 d. R, 3 d, p, 3 d, p, 3 d, p, 3 d, close r. Ch, 6 d, p, 6 d, p, 6 d. R, 3 d, join to 3rd p of last ring made, 3 d, join to center, 3 d, p, 3 d, close r. Ch, 6 d. R, 3 d, p, 3 d, p, 3 d, p, 3 d, close r. Ch, 6 d. R, 3 d, p, 3 d, p, 3 d, p, 3 d, close r. Ch, 6 d, p, 6 d, p, 6 d. R, 3 d, join to last p of last ring, 3 d, join to center p, 3 d, p, 3 d, close r. Ch, 6 d. R, 3 d, join to 2nd p of ch 6 of 2nd row over the 2 ring section, 3 d, p, 3 d, close r. R, 3 d, p, 3 d, join to p of ch 6 of 2nd row on the opposite side, 3 d, p, 3 d, close r. Ch, 6 d. R, 3 d, join to 3rd last ring made, 3 d, join to center p, 3 d, p, 3 d, close r. Ch, 6 d, p, 6 d, p, 6 d. R, 3 d, join to last p of last ring made, 3 d, join to center p, 3 d, join to 3rd p, 3 d, close r. Ch, 6 d. R, 3 d, p, 3 d, p, 3 d, close r. Ch, 6 d. R, 3 d, join to free p on opposite side, 3 d, join to center, 3 d, p, 3 d, close r. Ch, 6 d, p, 6 d, p, 6 d. R, 3 d, join to free p of last r, 3 d, join to center, 3 d, join to free p on opposite r, 3 d, close r. Ch, 6 d. R, 3 d, p, 3 d, p, 3 d, join to free p of ch, 3 d, close r. Ch, 6 d.

2nd Section of 3rd Row. This is made up and down and joined. R, 3 d, p, 3 d, p, 3 d, p, 3 d, close r. Ch, 6 d, p, 6 d, p, 6 d. R, 3 d, join to last r, 3 d, join to center, 3 d, p, 3 d, close r. Ch, 6 d, p, 6 d, p, 6 d. R, 3 d, join, 3 d, join to center, 3 d, p, 3 d, close r. Ch, 6 d, p, 6 d, p, 6 d. R, 3 d, join, 3 d, join to center, 3 d, join, 3 d, close r. Ch, 6 d. R, 3 d, join to last p of ch 6 loop, 3 d, p, 3 d, p, 3 d, close r. Ch, 6 d. R, 3 d, p, 3 d, p, 3 d, p, 3 d, close r. Ch, 6 d, p, 6 d, p, 6 d. R, 3 d, join to last r made, 3 d, join to center p, 3 d, p, 3 d, close r. Ch, 6 d. R, 3 d, p, 3 d, p, 3 d, p, 3 d, close r. Ch, 6 d, p, 3 d, p, 3 d, p, 3 d, close r. Ch, 6 d, join to last p of ch 6 loop, 6 d, p, 6 d. R, 3 d, join to last p of last ring made, 3 d, join to center p, 3 d, p, 3 d, close r. Ch,-6 d. R, 3 d, p, 3 d, join to the center p of r that joins the p of ch 6, 3 d, p, 3 d, close r. Ch, 6 d.

Continued on page 19.

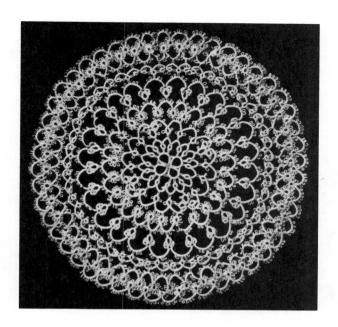

Fairy-Tale Doily

Materials Required—AMERICAN THREAD COMPANY "STAR" CROCHET COTTON, Size 30 or 50

2—150 Yd. Balls.
1 Tatting Shuttle.
Doily measures about 6½ inches.

Center. L R, 7 d, 6 p sep by 3 d, 7 d, close r. * L R, 7 d, join to 6th p of last r, 3 d, 5 p sep by 3 d, 7 d, close r. Repeat from * twice. Join last ring to first r, tie and cut thread in each row.

1st Row. * R, 4 d, join to p of L R, 4 d, close r, turn. Ch, 5 d, p, 5 d, turn, repeat from * all around.

2nd Row. S R, 3 d, 3 p sep by 3 d, 3 d, close r. L R, 3 d, join to 3rd p of last r, 3 d, p, 3 d, join to p of ch over center r, 3 d, 2 p sep by 3 d, 3 d, close r. S R, 3 d, join to 5th p of L R, 3 d, 2 p sep by 3 d, close r, turn. * Ch, 5 d, 3 p sep by 2 d, 5 d, turn. R, 3 d, p, 3 d, join to next picot of last row, 3 d, p, 3 d, close r, repeat from * twice, turn. Ch, 5 d, 3 p sep by 2 d, 5 d. Repeat from beginning all around.

3rd Row. * R, 4 p, join to center p of ch in previous row, 4 p, close r, turn. Ch, 5 d, 5 p sep by 2 d, 5 d, turn. R, 4 p, join to first p of next ch, 4 p, close r, turn. Ch, 5 d, 5 p sep by 2 d, 5 d, turn. R, 4 p, join to 3rd p of same ch, 4 p, close r, turn. Ch, 5 d, 5 p sep by 2 d, 5 d, turn. Repeat from * all around.

4th Row. * S R, 4 d, p, 4 d, close r. L R, 4 d, join to p of S R, 4 d, join to center p of ch in previous row, 4 d, p, 4 d, close r. S R, 4 d, join to 3rd p of L R, 4 d, close r, turn. Ch, 5 d, 5 p sep by 2 d, 5 d, turn. Repeat from * all around.

5th Row. S R, 2 d, p, 2 d, join to center p of ch in previous row, 2 d, p, 2 d, close r, * turn. Ch, 5 d, p, 5 d, turn. R, 2 d, p, 2 d, join to 3rd p of last r, 2 d, p, 2 d, close r. R, 2 d, 3 p sep by 2 d, 2 d, close r, turn. Ch, 5 d, p, 5 d, turn. R, 2 d, join to center p of last r, 2 d, join to center p of next ch, 2 d, p, 2 d, close r. Repeat from * all around.

6th Row. * R, 9 p, close r, turn. Ch, 5 d, 2 p sep by 2 d, join to p of ch in previous row, 2 d, 2 p sep by 2 d, 5 d, turn. Repeat from * all around.

7th Row. * R, 2 p, join to 7th p of r in previous row, 3 p, join to 3rd p of next r, 2 p, close r. Ch, 5 d, 5 p sep by 2 d, 5 d, turn. Repeat from * all around.

Enchanted Doily

Continued from page 18.

R, 3 d, p, 3 d, p, 3 d, p, 3 d, close r. Ch, 6 d, p, 6 d, p, 6 d. R, 3 d, join to last p of last r, 3 d, join to center p, 3 d, p, 3 d, close r. Ch, 6 d, p, 6 d, p, 6 d, p, 6 d. R, 3 d, join, 3 d, join to center, 3 d, p, 3 d, close r. Ch, 6 d, p, 6 d, p, 6 d. R, 3 d, join, 3 d, join to center, 3 d, join, 3 d, close r. Ch, 6 d. R, 3 d. join to last p of ch 6 loop, 3 d, join to the center p of the same r in the 3rd section, 3 d, p, 3 d, close r. Ch, 6 d. R, 3 d, join to free picot of r, 3 d, join to center, 3 d, p, 3 d, close r. Ch, 6 d, p, 6 d, join to the p of ch 6 loop of 1st section, 6 d. R, 3 d, join to last p of last r made, 3 d, join to center, 3 d, join to 3rd p, 3 d, close r. Ch, 6 d. R, 3 d, p, 3 d, join to p of 1st section, 3 d, p, 3 d, close r. Ch, 6 d. R, 3 d, join to free p of opposite r, 3 d, p, 3 d, p, 3 d, close r. Ch, 6 d, p, 3 d, join to 1st section, 6 d. R, 3 d, join to last p of last ring made, 3 d, join to center, 3 d, p, 3 d, close r. Ch, 6 d, join to the ch 6 loop of 2nd row, 6 d, join to the 2nd p, 6 d. R, 3 d, join to last p of last r, 3 d, join to center, 3 d, p, 3 d, close r. Continue up on other side to correspond and repeat 1st and 2nd sections of 3rd row all around.

19

Formal Lunch

**Materials Required—AMERICAN THREAD COMPANY
"STAR" MERCERIZED CROCHET COTTON,
Size 30**

6—150 Yd. Balls will make 4 doilies.
Each Doily measures about 8 x 14 inches.

R, 3 d, p, 3 d, p, 3 d, p, 3 d, close r, turn. Ch, 6 d, p, 6 d, p, 6 d, turn. R, 3 d, join to 3rd p of 1st ring made, 3 d, p, 3 d, p, 3 d, close r, turn. Ch, 6 d, p, 6 d, p, 6 d, turn. R, 3 d, join to 3rd p of last ring made, 3 d, join to center p, 3 d, p, 3 d, close r, turn. Ch, 6 d, turn. R, 3 d, p, 3 d, p, 3 d, p, 3 d, close r, turn. Ch, 6 d, turn. * R, 3 d, p, 3 d, p, 3 d, p, 3 d, close r, turn. Ch, 6 d, join to p of opposite ch, 6 d, p, 6 d, turn. R, 3 d, join to last p of last ring made, 3 d, join to center p, 3 d, p, 3 d, close r, turn. Ch, 6 d, p, 6 d, p, 6 d, turn. R, 3 d, join to last p of last ring made, 3 d, join to center p, 3 d, p, 3 d, close r, turn. Ch, 6 d, p, 6 d, p, 6 d, turn. R, 3 d, join to last p of last ring made, 3 d, join to center p, 3 d, join to 3rd p, 3 d, close r, turn. Ch, 6 d, turn. R, 3 d, join to 3rd p of single ring, 3 d,

join to center p, 3 d, p, 3 d, close r, turn. Ch, 6 d, turn. Repeat from * until there are 4 corners, joining the 4th corner to the 1st corner. Break thread and tie.
In joining motifs together, join the 4 p on the side of 2nd motif with the 4 p on the side of 1st motif, arranging the motifs as follows: starting at corner 1st row, 1 motif, 2nd row, 3 motifs, 3rd row, 5 motifs, 4th row, 7 motifs, 5th, 6th, 7th, 8th and 9th rows, 9 motifs, then decrease, 10th row, 7 motifs and so on until 1 motif remains.

Small Motifs. R, 3 d, p, 3 d, p, 3 d, p, 3 d, close r, turn. Ch, 6 d, p, 6 d, p, 6 d, turn. R, 3 d, join to 3rd p of 1st ring, 3 d, join to center p, 3 d, p, 3 d, close r, turn. Ch, 6 d, p, 6 d, join to 1st p of 2nd corner of large motif, 6 d, turn. R, 3 d, join to 3rd p of last ring made, 3 d, join to center p, 3 d, p, 3 d, close r, turn. Ch, 6 d, join to next p of same motif, 6 d, join to the 1st p of next motif, 6 d, turn. R, 3 d, join to 3rd p of last ring made, 3 d, join to center p, 3 d, join to 3rd p, close r, turn. Ch, 6 d, join to 2nd p of motif, 6 d, p, 6 d. Break thread and tie. Fill in all corners in same manner.

Picture Pretty Collar

Materials Required—AMERICAN THREAD COMPANY "STAR" MERCERIZED TATTING COTTON

4—75 Yd. Balls White or Colors.

Use 2 Shuttles or 1 Ball and 1 Shuttle.

Motif. * R, 4 d, p, 2 d, p, 4 d, p, 4 d, p, 2 d, p, 4 d, close r, turn. Ch, 4 d, 5 p sep by 2 d, 4 d, join to center p of r, turn and repeat from * 7 times, join to 1st r made.

Work a second motif joining it to 1st motif in the center p of 2 chs. Work 16 more motifs (or as many as desired), joining them in same manner. **2nd Row.** Work a motif joining it to next 2 free chs of 1st motif of 1st row. Work a second motif joining it to 1st motif in next free ch and to 1st row in next 2 free chs. Work 16 more motifs joining them in same manner. There should be 5 free chs at corner and 4 free chs at outer edge and 4 free loops at inside corner and 2 free loops on neck edge.

Outside Edge. 1st Row. Join thread to center p of 3rd free ch of corner and start work on short side. Ch, 4 d, 3 p sep by 4 d, 4 d, join to center p of next ch, 4 d, 3 p sep by 4 d, 4 d, turn. R, 4 d, join to 1st p of next ch, 3 d, join to last p of next ch, 4 d, close r, turn. Ch, 4 d, 3 p sep by 4 d, 4 d, join to center p of next ch, 4 d, 3 p sep by 4 d, 4 d, join to 2nd p of next ch, 4 d, 3 p sep by 4 d, 4 d, skip 1 p, join to next p, 4 d, 3 p sep by 4 d, 4 d, join to 2nd p of next ch, 4 d, 3 p sep by 4 d, 4 d, skip 1 p, join to next p, 4 d, 3 p sep by 4 d, 4 d, join to center p of next ch, 4 d, 3 p sep by 4 d, 4 d, join to center p of next ch, 4 d, turn. ** R, 4 d, join to 1st p of next ch, 3 d, join to last p of next ch, 4 d, close r. * Ch, 4 d, join to center p of next ch, 4 d, 3 p sep by 4 d, 4 d, join to center p of next ch, repeat from * twice, 4 d, repeat from ** to next corner and complete row to correspond.

On Neck Edge. * Ch, 4 d, 3 p sep by 4 d, 4 d, join to center p of next free ch, repeat from * to end of row and break thread.

2nd Row. Join thread in center p of last ch made, * ch, 4 d, 3 p sep by 4 d, 4 d, join to center p of next ch, repeat from * 3 times. Ch, 4 d, 3 p sep by 4 d, 4 d, turn. R, 4 d, p, 4 d, join to center p of next ch, 4 d, p, 4 d, cl r, turn. Ch, 4 d, 3 p sep by 4 d, 4 d, turn. R, 4 d, p, 4 d, join to same p as last r, 4 d, p, 4 d, cl r, turn. Ch, 4 d, 3 p sep by 4 d, 4 d, turn. R, 4 d, p, 4 d, join to center p of next ch, 4 d, p, 4 d, cl r, turn. Ch, 4 d, 3 p sep by 4 d, 4 d, turn. R, 4 d, p, 4 d, join to same p as last r, 4 d, p, 4 d, cl r, turn. Ch, 4 d, 3 p sep by 4 d, 4 d, join to center p of next ch. Ch, 4 d, 3 p sep by 4 d, 4 d, turn. R, 4 d, p, 4 d, join to center p of next ch, 4 d, p, 4 d, cl r, turn. Ch, 4 d, 3 p sep by 4 d, 4 d, turn. R, 4 d, p, 4 d, join to same p as last r, 4 d, p, 4 d, cl r, turn. Ch, 4 d, 3 p sep by 4 d, 4 d, join to center p of next ch. Ch, 4 d, 3 p sep by 4 d, 4 d, join to center p of next ch. * Ch, 4 d, 3 p sep by 4 d, 4 d, turn. R, 4 d, p, 4 d, join to center p of next ch, 4 d, p, 4 d, cl r, turn. Ch, 4 d, 4 p sep by 4 d, 4 d, turn. R, 4 d, p, 4 d, join in same p with last r, 4 d, p, 4 d, cl r, turn. Ch, 4 d, 3 p sep by 4 d, 4 d, join to center p of next ch. Ch, 4 d, 3 p sep by 4 d, join to center p of next ch. Repeat from * to corner working corner and side to correspond.

Around Neck Edge. Work chs of 3 d, 3 p sep by 3 d, 3 d, join to center p of ch in previous row.

Good Night, Ladies

Tatted Slip Top (top)

Materials Required—AMERICAN THREAD COMPANY "STAR" MERCERIZED TATTING COTTON

8—75 Yd. Balls White.

1 Shuttle and Ball.

2½ Yds. Narrow Ribbon.

R, * 1 d, p, repeat from * 11 times, (12 p) tie and cut.

2nd Row. R, 3 d, join to p of center r, 3 d, cl r. * Ch, 12 d. R, 2 d, 5 p sep by 2 d, 2 d, cl r. Ch, 12 d, turn. R, 3 d, join to next p of center r, 3 d, cl r, turn. Repeat from * 10 times. Ch, 12 d. R, 2 d, 5 p sep by 2 d, 2 d, cl r. Ch, 12 d, tie and cut.

3rd Row. R, 2 d, p, 2 d, join to 4th p of any r, 2 d, p, 2 d, join to 2nd p of next r, 2 d, p, 2 d, cl r, turn. Ch, 4 d, 5 p sep by 4 d, 4 d, turn. * R, 2 d, p, 2 d, join to 4th p of same r, 2 d, p, 2 d, join to 2nd p of next ring, 2 d, p, 2 d, cl r, turn. Ch, 4 d, 5 p sep by 4 d, 4 d, turn. Repeat from * all around.

Work a 2nd motif joining it to 1st motif in center p of 2 chs.

All motifs are joined in same manner.

Lower Edge. R, 4 d, 3 p sep by 4 d, 4 d, cl r, turn. ** Ch, 5 d. R, 3 d, p, 3 d, 3 p sep by 2 d, 3 d, p, 3 d, cl r, turn. Ch, 5 d. * R, 4 d, join to last p of opposite r, 4 d, p, 4 d, p, 4 d, cl r, turn. Ch, 5 d. R, 3 d, join to last p of opposite r, 3 d, 3 p sep by 2 d, 3 d, p, 3 d, cl r, turn. Ch, 5 d. Repeat from * 4 times. R, 4 d, join to last p of opposite r, 4 d, skip 1 free ch on motif, join to center p of next free ch, 4 d, p, 4 d, cl r, turn. Ch, 5 d. * R, 3 d, join to last p of opposite r, 3 d, 3 p sep by 2 d, 3 d, p, 3 d, cl r, turn. Ch, 5 d. R, 4 d, join to last p of opposite r, 4 d, p, 4 d, p, 4 d, cl r, turn. Ch, 5 d. Repeat from *. R, 3 d, join to last p of opposite r, 3 d, 3 p sep by 2 d, 3 d, p, 3 d, cl r, turn. Ch, 5 d. R, 4 d, join to last p of opposite r, 4 d, join to center p of next free ch, 4 d, p, 4 d, cl r, turn. Ch, 5 d. R, 3 d, join to last p of opposite r, 3 d, 3 p sep by 2 d, 3 d, p, 3 d, cl r, turn. Ch, 5 d. R, 4 d, join to last p of opposite r, 4 d, p, 4 d, p, 4 d, cl r, turn. Repeat from ** across each motif.

Beading at top is made same as lower edge having chs of 12 d between each r and joining to top of motifs in same manner.

Small joining Motif.

R, 3 d, p, 3 d, p, 3 d, cl r. Ch, 4 d. R, 4 d, join to 2nd p from top of free ch of large motif, 4 d, cl r, turn. Ch, 4 d, join to p of 1st r, 4 d. R, 4 d, join to 2nd p from top of next free ch of next large motif, 4 d, cl r. Ch, 4 d, join to next p of 1st ring, 4 d. R, 4 d join between 3rd and 4th free ring of lower edge, 4 d, cl r. Ch, 4 d, tie and cut.

Straps.

R, 4 d, 3 p sep by 4 d, 4 d, cl r, turn. Ch, 12 d. R, 4 d, 3 p sep by 4 d, 4 d, cl r, turn. * Ch, 12 d. R, 4 d, join to last p of opposite r, 4 d, p, 4 d, p, 4 d, cl r, turn. Repeat from * until strap measures 15 inches or length desired, tie and cut.

2nd Row. Join thread in center p of r. * Ch, 3 d, 3 p sep by 2 d, 3 d, join in center p of next r, repeat from * across row. Work other side of strap to correspond.

Lace ribbon through beading at top and also through straps.

Pointed Yoke (bottom)

Materials Required—AMERICAN THREAD COMPANY "STAR" MERCERIZED TATTING COTTON

3—75 Yd. Balls, White or Colors.

Use 2 Shuttles or 1 Shuttle and 1 Ball.

Motif. R, 1 d, 8 long picots sep by 1 d, 1 d, cl r, tie and cut.

2nd Row. * R, 4 d, join to p of center r, 4 d, cl r, turn. Ch, 4 d, 3 p sep by 2 d, 4 d, turn and repeat from * all around, tie and cut. Work a second motif joining it to 1st motif at center picots of 2 chs. Work a 3rd motif joining it in same manner leaving 2 free chs between joinings. Continue motifs until yoke is desired length. Work a second row of motifs joining them together and to 1st row in same manner.

To form points, work 5 motifs, then work 3 motifs and 1 motif. Allow 3 motifs between points for yoke size 34 to 36 and 4 motifs between points for larger size. Finish with ribbon straps.

WAVE YOUR MAGIC SHUTTLE AND CREATE THESE GOSSAMER

Table Settings

MATERIALS: J. & P. Coats or Clark's O.N.T. Best Six Cord Mercerized Crochet, *Size 30. White or Ecru—Small Ball:* J. & P. Coats—*124 balls*, or Clark's O.N.T. —*166 balls.*

Completed cloth measures 72 x 108 inches.

GAUGE: Each motif measures about 1¼ inches.

FIRST MOTIF . . . 1st rnd: R of 1 ds, 8 p's sep by 1 ds, 1 ds, cl. Tie and cut. Tie ball and shuttle threads together. **2nd rnd:** R of 3 ds, p, 3 ds, join to a p on 1st rnd, 3 ds, p, 3 ds, cl. * Rw, ch of 4 ds, p, 4 ds. Rw, r of 3 ds, join to p of adjacent r, 3 ds, join to next p on 1st rnd, 3 ds, p, 3 ds, cl. Repeat from * around, joining last part of last r to 1st p made and joining last ch to base of 1st r made. Tie and cut.

SECOND MOTIF . . . 1st rnd: Work same as 1st rnd of First Motif. **2nd rnd:** R of 3 ds, p, 3 ds, join to a p on 1st rnd, 3 ds, p, 3 ds, cl. * Rw, ch of 4 ds, join to p on ch on First Motif, 4 ds. Rw, r of 3 ds, join to p of adjacent r, 3 ds, join to next p on 1st rnd, 3 ds, p, 3 ds, cl. Repeat from * once more. Complete 2nd rnd same as 2nd rnd of First Motif (no more joinings).

Make 58 x 87 motifs, joining them as Second Motif was joined to First Motif.

BREAD TRAY DOILY. . . Page 27

24

A B C's

Materials Required—AMERICAN THREAD COMPANY "STAR" MERCERIZED CROCHET COTTON

Size 50, White.

1 Shuttle and 1 Ball.

A. R, 3 d, p, 3 d, p, 3 d, cl r. Ch, 5 d, p, 5 d. R, 6 d, s p, 6 d, cl r. Ch, 5 d, p, 8 d. R, 3 d, p, 3 d, cl r. Ch, 8 d, p, 8 d, join to s p of center r, 10 d. R, 8 d, p, 8 d, p, 8 d, cl r, tie and cut.

B. R, 4 d, p, 4 d, p, 4 d, p, 4 d, cl r. Ch, 4 d, s p, 10 d, s p, 8 d, turn. R, 3 d, 3 p sep by 3 d, 3 d, cl r. Ch, 5 d, 3 p sep by 5 d, 5 d, turn. R, 6 d, join to 2nd s p of ch, 6 d, cl r, turn. Ch, 5 d, 2 p sep by 5 d, 5 d. R, 5 d, p, 5 d, join to 1st s p of ch, 5 d, p, 6 d, cl r, tie and cut.

C. R, 8 d, p, 8 d, cl r. Ch, 16 d, join to p of r, 5 d, p, 10 d, p, 10 d, p, 10 d, p, 5 d, turn. R, 11 d, p, 10 d, cl r, tie and cut.

D. R, 2 d, 3 p sep by 2 d, 2 d, cl r. Ch, 6 d, p, 6 d, p, 6 d. R, 4 d, 3 p sep by 4 d, 4 d, cl r. Ch, 7 d, p, 7 d, p, 7 d, p, 7 d, p, 10 d, tie under 1st ring and cut.

E. R, 5 d, p, 5 d, p, 5 d, cl r. Ch, 9 d, p, 6 d. R, 2 d, 3 p sep by 2 d, 2 d, cl r. Ch, 9 d, p, 11 d, p, 11 d. R, 9 d, p, 8 d, p, 9 d, cl r, tie and cut.

F. R, 2 d, 3 p sep by 2 d, 2 d, cl r. Ch, 7 d. R, 5 d, p, 5 d, cl r. Ch, 11 d. R, 5 d, p, 5 d, cl r. Work another ring opposite same as last r. Ch, 14 d, p, 5 d, p, 7 d. R, 3 d, 3 p sep by 3 d, 3 d, cl r, tie and cut.

G. R, 8 d, p, 5 d, p, 8 d, cl r. Ch, 10 d, p, 10 d. R, 5 d, p, 4 d, p, 5 d, cl r. Ch, 16 d, p, 7 d, p, 6 d, join to p of last r, 8 d, join at 6th st from r, 7 d. R, 8 d, cl r, tie and cut.

H. R, 3 d, 3 p sep by 3 d, 3 d, cl r. Ch, 5 d, p, 5 d. R, 4 d, s p, 4 d, cl r. Ch, 5 d, p, 5 d. R, 3 d, 3 p sep by 3 d, 3 d, cl r, tie and cut. Work other half of letter in same manner joining the center rings at picots.

I. R, 5 d, p, 4 d, p, 4 d, p, 5 d, cl r. Ch, 8 d, p, 16 d, p, 6 d, p, 8 d, p, 7 d, join to 12th st of long ch, 4 d. R, 7 d, cl r, tie and cut.

J. R, 6 d, cl r. Ch, 12 d, p, 20 d, tie at 3rd st of ch from r, 14 d, p, 14 d, p, 12 d, tie in 3rd st of ch from center, 3 d, tie and cut.

K. R, 3 d, 3 p sep by 3 d, 3 d, cl r. Ch, 9 d. R, 3 d, p, 3 d, cl r. Ch, 8 d. R, 3 d, 3 p sep by 3 d, 3 d, cl r, tie and cut. **Second half.** R, 3 d, 3 p sep by 3 d, 3 d, cl r. Ch, 10 d, p, 9 d, join to p of center r of 1st half, 8 d, p, 7 d. R, 3 d, 3 p sep by 3 d, 3 d, cl r, tie and cut.

L. R, 3 d, 3 p sep by 3 d, 3 d, cl r. Ch, 12 d, p, 9 d. R, 6 d, p, 7 d, p, 6 d, cl r. Ch, 9 d. R, 4 d, 3 p sep by 4 d, 4 d, cl r, tie and cut.

M. R, 4 d, 3 p sep by 4 d, 4 d, cl r. Ch, 10 d, p, 10 d. R, 3 d, p, 3 d, cl r. Ch, 18 d. R, 6 d, cl r. Ch, 19 d. R, 3 d, p, 3 d, cl r. Ch, 10 d, p, 10 d. R, 4 d, 3 p sep by 4 d, 4 d, cl r, tie and cut.

N. R, 6 d, p, 6 d, p, 6 d, cl r. Ch, 10 d, p, 10 d. R, 3 d, p, 3 d, cl r. Ch, 21 d. R, 3 d, p, 3 d, cl r. Ch, 8 d, p, 8 d. R, 5 d, p, 5 d, p, 5 d, cl r, tie and cut.

O. R, 14 d, cl r. Ch, 10 d, p, 10 d, p, 10 d. R, 14 d, cl r. Ch, 10 d, p, 10 d, p, 10 d, tie to beginning of 1st ring and cut.

P. R, 6 d, p, 6 d, p, 6 d, cl r. Ch, 14 d, s p 8 d, s p, 3 d. R, 4 d, p, 4 d, p, 4 d, cl r, turn. Ch, 9 d, p, 9 d, p, 10 d, join to 1st s p of ch, 8 d. R, 3 d, join to next s p of ch, 3 d, cl r, tie and cut.

Q. R, 5 d, p, 5 d, p, 5 d, cl r. Ch, 5 d. R, 6 d, p, 6 d, p, 6 d, cl r, turn. Ch, 5 d, join to 2nd p of 1st r, 8 d, p, 11 d, p, 8 d. R, 10 d, p, 8 d, p, 10 d, cl r, tie and cut.

R. R, 4 d, p, 4 d, p, 4 d, cl r. Ch, 6 d, p, 7 d, s p, 8 d. R, 6 d, p, 6 d, cl r. Ch, 12 d, p, 8 d. R, 7 d, join to 2nd p of ch, 7 d, cl r. Ch, 13 d. R, 4 d, p, 4 d, p, 4 d, cl r, tie and cut.

S. R, 6 d, p, 6 d, p, 6 d, cl r. Ch, 9 d, p, 8 d, p, 6 d, turn ch, 9 d, p, 4 d, p, 9 d, tie where ch is turned to form top loop of letter, 6 d, p, 6 d, p, 6 d. R, 8 d, cl r, tie and cut.

T. R, 5 d, p, 5 d, cl r. Ch, 7 d. R, 3 d, p, 3 d, p, 3 d, cl r. Ch, 10 d, p, 10 d, p, 10 d. R, 5 d, p, 6 d, p, 5 d, cl r, tie and cut.

U. R, 4 d, 3 p sep by 4 d, 4 d, cl r. Ch, 6 d, join to side

p of r, 8 d, p, 7 d, p, 7 d. R, 11 d, cl r. Ch, 16 d. R, 8 d, cl r, tie and cut. Tie thread at 9th st from last r. Ch, 8 d. R, 3 d, p, 3 d, p, 3 d, cl r, tie and cut.

V. R, 3 d, 3 p sep by 3 d, 3 d, cl r. Ch, 5 d, join to side p of r, 10 d, p, 6 d, p, 6 d, turn. R, 6 d, p, 6 d, cl r. Ch, 7 d, p, 8 d. R, 4 d, p, 4 d, cl r. Ch, 5 d. R, 5 d, cl r, tie and cut.

W. R, 5 d, p, 5 d, p, 5 d, p, 5 d, cl r. Ch, 5 d, turn, join to side p of r, 8 d. R, 4 d, p, 3 d, p, 4 d, cl r. Ch, 7 d, turn. R, 5 d, p, 5 d, cl r. Ch, 7 d. R, 4 d, p, 3 d, p, 4 d, cl r. Ch, 15 d. R, 5 d, p, 5 d, p, 5 d, cl r, tie and cut.

X. R, 4 d, p, 5 d, p, 5 d, p, 4 d, cl r. Ch, 5 d, join to 1st p of r, 8 d, turn, 10 d. R, 3 d, p, 4 d, p, 4 d, p, 3 d, cl r, tie and cut. **Second half.** R, 5 d, p, 5 d, p, 5 d, cl r. Ch, 6 d, tie where ch is turned on 1st half, 9 d. R, 5 d, p, 5 d, p, 5 d, cl r, tie and cut.

Y. R, 5 d, 3 p sep by 5 d, 5 d, cl r. Ch, 7, join to side p of r, 10 d. R, 4 d, p, 4 d, cl r. Ch, 20 d. R, 8 d, cl r, tie and cut. Tie thread at 15th st of ch, 3 d, s p. 15 d, p, 10 d, join to s p of ch, 3 d. R, 5 d, cl r, tie and cut.

Z. R, 5 d, 3 p sep by 5 d, 5 d, cl r. Ch, 7 d. R, 5 d, p, 5 d, cl r. Ch, 4 d. R, 6 d, cl r. Ch. 4 d. R, 6 d, cl r. Ch. 5 d, turn. R, 5 d, p, 5 d, cl r. Ch, 12 d. R, 3 d, 3 p sep by 3 d, 3 d, cl r, tie and cut.

BREAD TRAY DOILY

Illustrated on page 24.

MATERIALS: J. & P. Coats or Clark's O.N.T. Best Six Cord Mercerized Crochet, *Size 20, 2 balls of White.*

Doily measures about 6 x 11 inches.

1st rnd: Tie ball and shuttle threads together. R of 4 ds, lp, 4 ds, cl. * Rw, ch of (2 ds, p) twice, 2 ds. Rw, r of 4 ds, join to lp of 1st r, 4 ds, cl. Repeat from * once more—end made. Work long side as follows: ** Rw, ch of 3 ds, p, 3 ds. Rw, r of 4 ds, p, 4 ds, cl. Repeat from ** 9 more times. Rw, ch of 3 ds, p, 3 ds. Make other end as follows: Rw, ch of 4 ds, lp, 4 ds, cl. (Rw, ch of 2 ds, p, 2 ds, p, 2 ds; rw, r of 4 ds, join to lp of this end r, 4 ds, cl) twice. Work along opposite side as follows: Rw, ch of 3 ds, p, 3 ds. Rw, r of 4 ds,

join to corresponding p on long side of oval, 4 ds, cl. Continue thus across, joining last ch to base of 1st r. Tie and cut. **2nd rnd:** R of 4 ds, join to 1st p on 1st ch of previous rnd, 4 ds, cl. Rw, ch of (2 ds, p) twice, 2 ds. Rw, r of 4 ds, join to next p on same ch, 4 ds, cl. Rw, ch of (2 ds, p) twice, 2 ds. Rw, r of 4 ds, join to 1st p on next ch, 4 ds, cl. Rw, ch of (2 ds, p) twice, 2 ds. Rw, r of 4 ds, join to next p on same ch, 4 ds, cl—end completed. * Rw, ch of 3 ds, p, 3 ds. Rw, r of 4 ds, join to p on next ch, 4 ds, cl. Repeat from * across to opposite end. Work other end and opposite side to correspond, joining last ch to base of 1st r. Tie and cut. **3rd rnd:** R of 4 ds, join to 1st p on 1st ch of last rnd, 4 ds, cl. * Rw, ch of (2 ds, p) 3 times, 2 ds. Rw, r of 4 ds, join to next

p on same ch, 4 ds, cl. Rw, ch of (3 ds, p) twice, 3 ds. Rw, r of 4 ds, join to 1st p on next ch. Repeat from * 2 more times. ** Rw, ch of (2 ds, p) 3 times, 2 ds. Rw, r of 4 ds, join to p on next ch. Repeat from ** to opposite end. Work other end and opposite side to correspond, joining last ch to base of 1st r. Tie and cut. **4th rnd:** R of 2 ds, join to any p on 3rd rnd, 2 ds, cl. * Sp of 1 inch, r of 2 ds, join to next p, 2 ds, cl. Repeat from * around. Hereafter mark the end of each rnd. **5th rnd:** * Sp of 1 inch, r of 2 ds, join to thread between next 2 r's on previous rnd, 2 ds, cl. Repeat from * around. **6th to 9th rnds incl:** Repeat 5th rnd, making the sp between r's ¼ inch longer on each successive rnd. Tie and cut at end of 9th rnd. Starch and press.

Saturn Ring

MATERIALS: J. & P. Coats or Clark's O.N.T. Best Six Cord Mercerized Crochet, Size 30, 1 ball of White.

Doily measures about 7½ inches in diameter.

Tie ball and shuttle threads together. **1st rnd:** R of 10 ds, p, 10 ds, cl. (Rw, ch of 5 ds, 3 p's sep by 5 ds, 5 ds. Rw, r of 10 ds, join to p of preceding r, 10 ds, cl) 4 times. Ch of 5 ds, 3 p's sep by 5 ds, 5 ds. Join at base of first r. Tie and cut. **2nd rnd:** Attach thread to first p of first ch. * Ch of 5 ds, 3 p's sep by 5 ds, 5 ds, join to 3rd p of same ch. Ch of 5 ds, 3 p's sep by 5 ds, 5 ds, join to first p of next ch. Repeat from * around. Tie and cut. **3rd rnd:** Attach thread to center p of ch of preceding rnd. * Ch of 5 ds, 5 p's sep by 5 ds, 5 ds, join to center p of next ch. Repeat from * around. Tie and cut. **4th rnd:** Attach thread to 2nd p of ch of preceding rnd. * Ch of 3 ds, 5 p's sep by 3 ds, 3 ds, join to 4th p of same ch. Ch of 3 ds, 5 p's sep by 3 ds, 3 ds, join to 2nd p of next ch. Repeat from * around. Tie and cut. **5th rnd:** Attach thread to center p of ch of preceding rnd. * Ch of 4 ds, 5 p's sep by 3 ds, 4 ds, join to center p of next ch. Repeat from * around. Tie and cut. **6th rnd:** R of 5 ds, join to center p of ch of preceding rnd, 5 ds, cl. * Rw, ch of 12 ds. R of 5 ds, p, 5 ds, cl. Rw, ch of 12 ds. R of 5 ds, join to center p of next ch, 5 ds, cl. Repeat from * around. Tie and cut. **7th rnd:** R of 5 ds, join to free p of r of preceding rnd, * 5 ds, cl. Rw, ch of 5 ds, 5 p's sep by 5 ds, 5 ds. Rw, r of 5 ds, join to next free p. Repeat from * around. Tie and cut. **8th rnd:** Attach thread to 2nd p of ch of preceding rnd. * Ch of 3 ds, 5 p's sep by 3 ds, 3 ds, join to 4th p of same ch. Ch of 3 ds, 5 p's sep by 3 ds, 3 ds, join to 2nd p of next ch. Repeat from * around. Tie and cut. **9th rnd:** Attach thread to center p of ch of preceding rnd. * Ch of 4 ds, 5 p's sep by 4 ds, 4 ds, join to center p of next ch. Repeat from * around. Tie and cut.

Lover's Knot

MATERIALS: J. & P. Coats or Clark's O.N.T. Best Six Cord Mercerized Crochet, *Size 30, 1 ball of White.*

Doily measures 8 inches in diameter.

Tie ball and shuttle threads together. **1st rnd:** R of 4 ds, p, 4 ds, cl. (Rw, ch of 2 ds, 2 p's sep by 3 ds, 3 ds. Rw, r of 4 ds, join to p of preceding r, 4 ds, cl) 4 times. Rw, ch of 2 ds, 2 p's sep by 3 ds, 3 ds. Join to base of first r. Tie and cut. **2nd rnd:** R of 4 ds, join to any p of ch of preceding rnd, 4 ds, cl. * Sp of 3/8 inch. Rw, r of 2 ds, 2 p's sep by 3 ds, 2 ds, cl. Sp of 3/8 inch. Rw, r of 4 ds, join to next p, 4 ds, cl. Repeat from * around. Join to base of first r. Tie and cut. **3rd rnd:** R of 4 ds, join to first p of 2-p r of preceding rnd, 4 ds, cl. * Rw, ch of 3 ds, 2 p's sep by 3 ds, 3 ds. Rw, r of 4 ds, join to 2nd p of same r, 4 ds, cl. Rw, ch of 3 ds, 2 p's sep by 3 ds, 3 ds. Rw, r of 4 ds, join to first p of next r, 4 ds, cl. Repeat from * around. Tie and cut. **4th rnd:** R of 4 ds, join to first p of ch of preceding rnd, 4 ds, cl. * Rw, ch of 1 ds, 2 lp's sep by 3 ds, 1 ds. Rw, r of 4 ds, join to 2nd p of same ch, 4 ds, cl. Rw, ch of 1 ds, 3 lp's sep by 2 ds, 1 ds. Rw, r of 4 ds, join to first p of next ch, 4 ds, cl. Repeat from * around. Tie and cut. **5th rnd:** Sm r of 2 ds, join to any p of ch of preceding rnd, 2 ds, cl. * Sp of 1/2 inch, sm r of 2 ds, join to next p, 2 ds, cl. Repeat from * around. Hereafter mark the end of each rnd. **6th rnd:** * Sp of 1/2 inch, r of 2 ds, join to thread between next 2 r's of preceding rnd, 2 ds, cl. Repeat from * around. **7th, 8th and 9th rnds:** Work as for 6th rnd, only making the sp between r's 3/4 inch instead of 1/2 inch. Tie and cut at end of 9th rnd. Starch lightly and press.

Beauty for Baby

The Cap

Infant Size

Materials: J. & P. Coats Tatting Cotton, 3 balls.
A shuttle.
1½ yds. of ribbon 1 inch wide.

Center Medallion. 1st rnd: R of 1 ds, lp, * 2 ds, lp. Repeat from * 8 more times, ds, cl. Fasten and break off. **2nd rnd:** R of 2 ds, join to 1st lp of r just made, 2 ds, cl. Rw, ** sp (⅛-inch). Lr of * 3 ds, p. Repeat from * 4 more times, 3 ds, cl. Rw, sp (⅛-inch), r of 2 ds, join to next lp of 1st rnd, 2 ds, cl. Rw. Repeat from ** around. Fasten and break off. **3rd rnd:** R of 3 ds, p, 3 ds, join to center p of previous rnd, 3 ds, p, 3 ds, cl. Rw, sp (⅛-inch). lr of 3 ds, 5 p's sep. by 3 ds, 3 ds, cl. Rw. * Sp (⅛-inch), sr of 3 ds, join to last p of previous sr, 3 ds, join to same p where last sr was joined, 3 ds, p, 3 ds, cl. Rw, sp (⅛-inch), lr of 3 ds, join to last p of previous lr, 3 ds, 4 p's sep. by 3 ds, 3 ds,

cl. Rw, sp (⅛-inch), sr of 3 ds, join to last p of previous sr, 3 ds, join to next center p of next r, 3 ds, p, 3 ds, cl. Rw, sp (⅛-inch), lr of 3 ds, join to last p of previous lr, 3 ds, 4 p's sep. by 3 ds, 3 ds, cl. Rw. Repeat from * around, joining the last lr to adjacent p's at both sides. Fasten and break off.

Small Medallions. 1st rnd: Repeat 1st and 2nd rnds of center medallion, but having 8 lp's (instead of 10 lp's) in the rnd, and joining center p of one lr to center p of one lr of center medallion. Make 9 more medallions in same way, joining to center p of every other r of center medallion and joining by center p's of 2 r's (adjacent to r joining center medallion), thus leaving 3 r's free on outer edge of this rnd. **2nd rnd:** Repeat 1st and 2nd rnds of center medallion, but having 12 lp's (instead of 10 lp's) in the rnd, and joining center p's of 2 lr's to center p's of 2 lr's (adjacent to r joining 2nd rnd), then join following 2 lr's to 2 lr's on next medallion (adjacent to r joining 2nd rnd); then complete rnd (thus a medallion is joined between 2 medallions of 2nd rnd—this is center back). Make another medallion as before, but joining center 3 p's to center 3 p's of center back medallion (adjacent to r joining 2nd rnd); then join next center p to next center p of same medallion and complete rnd. Make 10 more medallions, joining 3 p's to previous medallion as before; then join center p of next lr to center p of next lr where last p was joined to 2nd rnd. Then join next center p to next center p of next medallion. Continue in this manner around, but leave one lr free at center of each medallion of 2nd rnd. **3rd rnd:** Repeat medallions as for 2nd rnd, but having 2 joinings on 1st and 2nd medallions of previous rnd. Continue in this manner around until 10 medallions are in the rnd, making 2 joinings on previous medallion made and on each of next 2 medallions. **4th rnd:** R of 3 ds, join to center p of 3rd r from joining, 4 p's sep. by 3 ds, 3 ds, cl. * Sp (¼-inch), r of 3 ds, join to last p of previous r made, 3 ds, 4 p's sep. by 3 ds, 3 ds, cl. Repeat from * until 6 r's are made, but joining the last r at p's on both sides. Then draw thread through center sp and tie securely (thus a fill-in cluster is made). Hereafter make medallions as for previous rnd and joining 2 r's to fill-in cluster and to each of next 2 medallions. Finish rnd with another fill-in cluster. **5th rnd:** Same as 3rd rnd, but making only 1 joining at fill-in clusters.

Insertion. R of 2 ds, lp, 2 ds, joining to center p of 4th r from joining, 2 ds, lp, 2 ds, cl. Rw, sp (⅛-inch), r of 2 ds, 3 lp's sep. by 2 ds, 2 ds, cl. Rw, sp (⅛-inch), r of 2 ds, join to last p of 1st r made, 2 ds, lp, 2 ds, lp, 2 ds, cl. Rw, sp (⅛-inch). Continue in this manner, joining every other r on inner edge to 3 free r's of each medallion, making r between each joining and 2 r's between each medallion.

Sew ends of ribbon, one on each side of lower edge. Cut ribbon in center, and tie.

The Bootees

Infant Size

Materials: J. & P. Coats Tatting Cotton, 2 balls.
A shuttle.
1 yd. ribbon ½-inch wide.

1st rnd: Starting at sole, make r of 3 ds, 5 p's sep. by 3 ds, 3 ds, cl. Sp (⅛-inch), r of 3 ds, join to last p of previous r, 3 ds, 4 p's sep. by 3 ds, 3 ds, cl. Rw. Sp (⅛-inch), r of 3 ds, join to 1st p at opposite side of 1st r, 3 ds, 4 p's sep. by 3 ds, cl. * Rw. Sp (⅛-inch), r of 3 ds, join to last p of r at opposite side. Repeat from * until there are 10 r's on both sides, then make another r as before, but joining at both sides at 1st and last p's. Tie securely. Break off. **2nd rnd:** R of 3 ds, p, 3 ds, p, 3 ds, join to center p of 1st r made in previous rnd, 3 ds, p, 3 ds, p, 3 ds, cl. Rw, sp (¼-inch). R of 3 ds, 5 p's sep. by 3 ds, 3 ds, cl. Rw, sp (¼-inch). R of 3 ds, join to 1st p of 1st r made, 3 ds, p, 3 ds, join to same p where last r was joined, 3 ds, p, 3 ds, p, 3 ds, cl (1 r increased). Rw. Hereafter continue as for 1st rnd, but joining center p of each r on one side to center p of each r of previous rnd, and making another increase as before at opposite end. Join last r at both sides at 1st and last p's.

Toe. Count off the center 8 r's at one end of sole and mark with a pin. Then work over these 8 r's as for 1st rnd, joining center p of one side to center p of adjacent r (thus forming toe).

Medallion. Starting at center, make r of 1 ds, lp, * 2 ds, lp. Repeat from * 10 more times, 1 ds, cl. (12 lp's in rnd). Tie securely and break off. Sr of 3 ds, join to lp of r just made, 3 ds, cl. Rw, sp (¼-inch), lr of 3 ds, p, 3 ds, p, 3 ds, skip end r of toe, join to center p of next r (next to toe end), 3 ds, p, 3 ds, p, 3 ds, cl. Rw, sp (¼-inch), sr of 3 ds, join to next p of center r, 3 ds, cl. Rw, sp (¼-inch), lr of 3 ds, join to p of lr made previously, 3 ds, p, 3 ds, join to center p of next toe r, 3 ds, p, 3 ds, p, 3 ds, cl. Rw, sp (¼-inch), sr same as before, join to next p of center r. Rw, sp (¼-inch), lr of 3 ds, join to last p of previous lr, 3 ds, join to next r of toe, 3 ds, join to next r of toe, 3 ds, join to next r of toe, 3 ds, p, 3 ds, cl. Rw. Continue thus around, joining center p's of next 2 lr's to center p's of next 2 r's of toe, and complete rnd, alternating lr's and sr's as before. Make 5 more medallions, joining center p's of 3 r's to adjacent p's of previous medallion and joining center p's of 3 r's to adjacent p's on sole, leaving a lr free between medallions on sole.

Beading. 1st rnd: R of 2 ds, 3 p's sep. by 2 ds, 2 ds, cl. ** Rw, sp (⅛-inch), r of 4 ds, p, 4 ds, cl. Rw, sp (¼-inch), r of 2 ds, join to last p of 1st r made, 2 ds, p, 2 ds, p, 2 ds, cl. Rw, sp (¼-inch), r of 4 ds, join to last p of adjacent r, 4 ds, cl. Rw, sp (¼-inch), r of 2 ds, join to last p of previous r, 2 ds, p, 2 ds, p, 2 ds, cl. Repeat from ** around, joining to center p's of r's in each medallion. Break off. **2nd rnd:** * R of 4 ds, p, 4 ds, cl. Rw, r of 4 ds, join to center p of each of 2 r's of previous rnd, 4 ds, cl. Rw, r of 4 ds, p, 4 ds, cl. Rw, r of 4 ds, join to same p's as last r was joined, 4 ds, cl. Rw. Repeat from * around. Fasten and break off.

Run ribbon through beading, and tie.

Lyric Luncheon Set

Materials Required: AMERICAN THREAD COMPANY "STAR" MERCERIZED CROCHET COTTON, Article 20, Size 50, 11 balls White **or**
"GEM" MERCERIZED CROCHET COTTON, Article 35, Size 50, 9 balls White.

96 Motifs 8 x 12 are required for Center Mat measuring about 17 x 26½ inches.

48 Motifs 6 x 8 are required for each Plate Mat measuring about 13 x 17 inches.

1 Shuttle and 1 Ball.

MOTIF—R, 3 d, 4 p sep by 3 d, 3 d, cl r. R, 3 d, join to last p of last r made, 3 d, 4 p sep by 3 d, 3 d, cl r. R, 3 d, join to last p of last r made, 3 d, 3 p sep by 3 d, 3 d, cl r (clover), turn. Ch, 6 d, small p, 3 d, small p, 6 d, turn. * R, 3 d, p, 3 d, join to center free p of last r made, 3 d, 2 p sep by 3 d, 3 d, cl r. R, 3 d, join to last p of last r made, 3 d, 4 p sep by 3 d, 3 d, cl r. R, 3 d, join to last p of last r made, 3 d, 3 p sep by 3 d, 3 d, cl r, turn. Ch, 6 d, join to last p of previous ch, 3 d, small p, 6 d, turn. Repeat from * twice joining the last r to 1st r made and joining the ch at corresponding picots, tie and cut.

2nd Row—R, 4 d, 4 p sep by 4 d, 4 d, cl r, * turn. Ch, 6 d, turn. R, 4 d, p, 4 d, join to last p of last r made, 4 d, 2 p sep by 4 d, 4 d, cl r. R, 4 d, join to last p of last r made, 4 d, 4 p sep by 4 d, 4 d, cl r. R, 4 d, join to last p of last r made, 4 d, 3 p sep by 4 d, 4 d, cl r, turn. Ch, 6 d, turn. R, 4 d, join to center free p of last r made, 4 d, 3 p sep by 4 d, 4 d, cl r, turn. Ch, 6 d, p, 6 d, join to p of 1st r of clover of 1st row, 6 d, join to 1st p of next r of same clover of 1st row, 6 d, p, 3 d, turn. R, 4 d, p, 4 d, join to center free p of last r made, 4 d, 2 p sep by 4 d, 4 d, cl r. R, 4 d, join to last p of last r made, 3 d, 4 p sep by 3 d, 4 d, cl r. R, 4 d, join to last p of last r made, 4 d, 3 p sep by 4 d, 4 d, cl r, turn. Ch, 3 d, join to last p of last ch, 6 d, skip 1 p of same r of 1st row, join in next p, 6 d, join to next p of next r of same clover, 6 d, p, 6 d, turn. R, 4 d, p, 4 d, join to center free p of last r made, 4 d, 2 p sep by 4 d, 4 d, cl r. Repeat from * twice, turn. Ch, 6 d, turn. R, 4 d, p, 4 d, join to last p of last r made, 4 d, 2 p sep by 4 d, 4 d, cl r. R, 4 d, join to last p of last r made, 4 d, 4 p sep by 4 d, 4 d, cl r. R, 4 d, join to last p of last r made, 4 d, 3 p sep by 4 d, 4 d, cl r, turn. Ch, 6 d, turn. R, 4 d, join to center free p of last r made, 4 d, 3 p sep by 4 d, 4 d, cl r, turn. Ch, 6 d, join to opposite p of last ch, 6 d, join to next p of next r of 1st row, 6 d, join to next p of next r of same clover of 1st row, 6 d, p, 3 d, turn. R, 4 d, p, 4 d, join to center free p of last r made, 4 d, 2 p sep by 4 d, 4 d, cl r. R, 4 d, join to last p of last r made, 3 d, 4 p sep by 3 d, 4 d, cl r. R, 4 d, join to last p of last r made, 4 d, p, 4 d, join to center free p of 1st row made, 4 d, p, 4 d, cl r, turn. Ch, 3 d, join to opposite p of last ch, 6 d, skip 1 p, join in next p of same r of same clover, 6 d, join to next p of next r of same clover, 6 d, join to top of opposite ch, 6 d, tie and cut. Join 2nd motif to 1st motif in last row as follows: R, 4 d, 4 p sep by 4 d, 4 d, cl r, turn. Ch, 6 d, turn. R, 4 d, p, 4 d, join to last p of last r made, 4 d, 2 p sep by 4 d, 4 d, cl r. R, 4 d, join to last p of last r made, 4 d, 2 p sep by 4 d, 4 d, join to corresponding p of 1st motif, 4 d, p, 4 d, cl r. R, 4 d, join to last p of last r made, 4 d, 3 p sep by 4 d, 4 d, cl r, turn. R, 4 d, join to center free p of last r made, 4 d, 3 p sep by 4 d, 4 d, cl r, turn. Ch, 6 d, p, 6 d, join to p of 1st r of clover of 1st row, 6 d, join to 1st p of next r of same clover, 6 d, p, 3 d, turn. R, 4 d, p, 4 d, join to center free p of last r made, 4 d, 2 p sep by 4 d, 4 d, cl r. R, 4 d, join to last p of last r made, 3 d, p, 3 d, join to center p of corresponding r of 1st motif, 3 d, p, 3 d, 4 d, cl r. R, 4 d, join to last p of last r made, 4 d, 3 p sep by 4 d, 4 d, cl r. Ch, 3 d, join to p of opposite ch, 6 d, skip 1 p, join to next p of same r of same clover, 6 d, join to next p of next r of same clover, 6 d, p, 6 d, turn. R, 4 d, p, 4 d, join to center free p of last r made, 4 d, 2 p sep by 4 d, 4 d, cl r, turn. Ch, 6 d, turn. R, 4 d, p, 4 d, join to last p of last r made, 4 d, 2 p sep by 4 d, 4 d, cl r. R, 4 d, join to last p of last r made, 4 d, join to corresponding p of 1st motif, 4 d, 3 p sep by 4 d, 4 d, cl r and complete motif same as 1st motif. Join all motifs in same manner.

Cross Bookmark

Quantity: 1 ball White and 1 ball Color desired.

1 Shuttle and 1 Ball.

MOTIF: WITH COLOR—R, 4 d, 3 p sep by 4 d, 4 d, cl r. * R, 4 d, join to last p of last r made, 4 d, p, 4 d, p, 4 d, cl r. Repeat from * 4 times joining last p of last r to 1st p of 1st r, tie and cut.

2nd Motif—R, 4 d, p, 4 d, join to center p of any r of 1st motif, 4 d, p, 4 d, cl r. R, 4 d, join to last p of last r, 4 d, join to center p of next r of 1st motif, 4 d, p, 4 d, cl r. * R, 4 d, join to last p of last r, 4 d, p, 4 d, cl r. Repeat from * 3 times joining last p of last r to 1st p of 1st r, tie and cut. These 2 motifs are used for top of cross. Work 2 more groups of 2 motifs in same manner for each arm. Work 6 motifs for lower end or stem of cross joining in same manner and leaving 1 r free on either side of motif.

Lay the 2 motifs for top, 2 motifs for each arm and 6 motifs for lower end on table in position to be joined together.

With White thread in shuttle: R, 8 d, join to free p of upper left hand r of stem, 2 d, p, 2 d, join to center p of lower right hand r of left arm leaving 1 r free, 8 d, cl r. R, 8 d, join to center p of next r of left arm, 2 d, p, 2 d, join to center p of lower left hand r of top, 8 d, cl r. R, 8 d, join to center p of next r of top, 2 d, p, 2 d, skip 1 r, join to center p of next r of right arm, 8 d, cl r. R, 8 d, join to center p of next r of right arm, 2 d, p, 2 d, join to center p of upper right hand r of stem, 8 d, cl r, tie and cut.

BORDER—Using shuttle and ball of Color desired, work around entire cross as follows: attach thread in 1st free picot from joining on left hand side at lower edge of stem and working up the left side, ch, 8 d, turn. R, 4 d, join to p which connects the 2 lower motifs, 4 d, cl r, turn. * Ch, 8 d, join to free p of 2nd motif. Ch, 8 d, turn. R, 4 d, join to p which connects the next 2 motifs, 4 d, cl r, turn. Repeat from * 3 times. Ch, 8 d, join to free p of next r of next motif. Ch, 4 d, turn. R, 5 d, join to free p of large White ring, 5 d, cl r, turn. Ch, 4 d, join to 1st free p of left arm. Ch, 8 d, turn. R, 4 d, join to p which connects the 2 motifs of left arm, 4 d, cl r, turn. Ch, 8 d, join to free p of next r of same motif. Ch, 11 d, join to free p of next r of same motif. Ch, 12 d, join to free p of next r of same motif. Ch, 11 d, join to free p of next r of same motif. Ch, 8 d, turn. R, 4 d, join to p connecting the 2 motifs of left arm, 4 d, cl r, turn. Ch, 8 d, join to free p of next r, 4 d, turn. R, 5 d, join to free p of large White ring, 5 d, cl r, turn. Ch, 4 d, join to 1st free p of next motif of top of cross, 8 d, turn. R, 4 d, join to p that connects the next 2 motifs of top of cross, 4 d, cl r, turn. Ch, 8 d, join to free p of next r of top motif. Ch, 11 d, join to next free p of next r of same motif. Ch, 12 d, join to next free p of next r of same motif. Ch, 11 d c, join to next p of next r of same motif. Ch, 8 d, finish opposite side to correspond working lower edge same as top, tie and cut.

TASSEL—Cut 35 lengths about 3½ inches long in Colors desired. Double in half and tie. Tie again about ¼ inch from top.

CORD—Crochet a ch about 3 inches long, s c in 2nd st from hook, 1 s c in each remaining st of ch. Fasten to lower edge of cross. Sew tassel in position as illustrated.

Summer Evening

MATERIALS: J. & P. Coats or Clark's O.N.T. Best Six Cord Mercerized Crochet, *Size 30.*

MOTIF . . . 1st rnd: R of 1 ds, 7 p's sep by 1 ds, 1 ds, cl. Leave sp on the threads equivalent in length to a picot (thereby making the 8th p). Tie and cut. **2nd rnd:** Tie ball and shuttle threads together. R of 8 ds, sm p, 6 ds, join to 8th p of 1st rnd, 6 ds, sm p, 8 ds, cl. * Rw, ch of 3 ds, 5 p's sep by 3 ds, 3 ds. Rw, r of 11 ds, join to last sm p of preceding r, 3 ds, p, 3 ds, sm p, 11 ds, cl. Rw, ch of 3 ds, 5 p's sep by 3 ds, 3 ds. Rw, r of 8 ds, join to sm p of preceding r, 6 ds, skip next p on 1st rnd, join to next p, 6 ds, sm p, 8 ds, cl. Repeat from * twice. Rw, make another ch. Rw, r of 11 ds, join to sm p of preceding r, 3 ds, p, 3 ds, join to sm p of 1st r, 11 ds, cl. Rw, make another ch and fasten at base of 1st r. Tie and cut. These 2 rnds complete motif. **Next rnd:** Tie ball and shuttle threads together, r of 3 ds, 9 p's sep by 3 ds, 3 ds, cl. Rw, ch of 3 ds, 6 p's sep by 3 ds, 3 ds. * Rw, r of 3 ds, push threads apart beneath last p on preceding ch and join loosely to that sp, 3 ds, 8 p's sep by 3 ds, 3 ds, cl. Rw, r of 3 ds, join to last p of preceding ch, 3 ds, 3 p's sep by 3 ds, 3 ds, join to 3rd p on next ch of motif, 3 ds, 4 p's sep by 3 ds, 3 ds, cl. Rw, r of 3 ds, join to last p of next-to-last r, 3 ds, 8 p's sep

by 3 ds, 3 ds, cl. Rw, ch of 3 ds, fasten to last p of preceding r, then join to last p of next-to-last r, 3 ds, 5 p's sep by 3 ds, 3 ds. Rw, r of 3 ds, 9 p's sep by 3 ds, 3 ds, cl. Rw, ch of 3 ds, join to last p of preceding ch, 3 ds, 5 p's sep by 3 ds, 3 ds. Repeat from * around, joining the last p of the last ch to the 1st p of the 1st ch and fastening it at the base of the 1st r. Tie and cut. **Following rnd:** Fasten ball and shuttle threads to 5th free p on 1st r of 3-r group on preceding rnd. Ch of 3 ds, 4 p's sep by 3 ds, 3 ds, fasten to 3rd free p of next r of same group. * Ch of 3 ds, join to last p of preceding ch, 3 ds, 8 p's sep by 3 ds, 3 ds, fasten to 5th p of next single r on preceding rnd. Ch of 3 ds, 9 p's sep by 3 ds, 3 ds, fasten to 5th p of 1st r of next 3-r group. Ch of 3 ds, join to last p of preceding ch, 3 ds, 3 p's sep by 3 ds, 3 ds, fasten to 3rd p of next r and repeat from * around, joining the last p of the last ch to the 1st p of the 1st ch and fastening last ch to p from which rnd started. Tie and cut.

Next rnd: This rnd is made up of 8 Motifs joined to preceding rnd as follows: Work the 1st rnd of Motif. **2nd rnd:** Tie ball and shuttle threads together. R of 8 ds, sm p, 6 ds, join to 8th p of 1st rnd, 6 ds, sm p, 8 ds, cl. Rw, ch of 3 ds, 5 p's sep by 3 ds, 3 ds. Rw, r of 11 ds, join to last sm p of pre-

ceding r, 3 ds, p, 3 ds, sm p, 11 ds, cl. Rw, ch of 3 ds, p, 3 ds, join to 4th p of last ch of preceding rnd, 3 ds, join to 5th p of same ch, (3 ds, p) twice, 3 ds. Rw, r of 8 ds, join to last sm p of preceding r, 6 ds, skip next p, join to next p of 1st rnd, 6 ds, sm p, 8 ds, cl. Rw, ch of (3 ds, p) twice, 3 ds, join to 4th free p of next ch of preceding rnd, 3 ds, join to next p of same ch, 3 ds, p, 3 ds. Rw and complete motif same as before with no more joinings. Make and join 7 more motifs same as this. **Last rnd:** Tie ball and shuttle threads together, * r of (3 ds, p) twice, 3 ds, join to center p on next ch of a motif, (3 ds, p) twice, 3 ds, cl. Rw, ch of 3 ds, 4 p's sep by 3 ds, 3 ds, sm p, 3 ds. Rw, r of 12 ds, sm p, 3 ds, cl. R of 3 ds, join to p of preceding r, 6 ds, p, 6 ds, sm p, 3 ds, cl. R of 3 ds, join to sm p of preceding r, 12 ds, cl (clover made). Rw, ch of 3 ds, join to sm p of preceding ch, 3 ds, join to 4th p of same ch, 3 ds, 3 p's sep by 3 ds, 3 ds. Rw, r of (3 ds, p) twice, 3 ds, skip 1 ch on next motif, join to 3rd p of next ch, (3 ds, p) twice, 3 ds, cl. Rw, ch of 3 ds, 13 p's sep by 3 ds, 3 ds. Rw, r of 15 ds, join to 3rd p on next ch of same motif, 15 ds, cl. Rw, ch of 3 ds, 13 p's sep by 3 ds, 3 ds. Rw, r of 15 ds, join to 3rd p on next ch of same motif, 15 ds, cl. Rw, ch of 3 ds, 13 p's sep by 3 ds, 3 ds. Rw, repeat from * around doily. Tie and cut.

Cobweb Doily

MATERIALS: J. & P. Coats or Clark's O.N.T. Best Six Cord Mercerized Crochet, *Size 30, 1 ball of Pastels.*

Doily measures about 8 inches in diameter.

STAR . . . Tie ball and shuttle threads together. R of 4 ds, lp, 4 ds, cl. * Rw, ch of 2 ds, p, 3 ds, p, 2 ds. Rw, r of 4 ds, join to lp of 1st r, 4 ds, cl. Repeat from * 3 more times. Rw, ch of 2 ds, p, 3 ds, p, 2 ds. Join to base of 1st r. Tie and cut. **1st rnd:** R of 4 ds, join to any p of Star, 4 ds, cl. * Rw, ch of 2 ds, lp, 3 ds, lp, 2 ds. Rw, r of 4 ds, join to next p on Star, 4 ds, cl. Repeat from * around, joining last ch to base of 1st r. Tie and cut. **2nd rnd:** R of 4 ds, join to any p on 1st rnd, 4 ds, cl. * Rw, ch of 4 ds, p, 4 ds. Rw, r of 4 ds, join to next p on previous rnd, 4 ds, cl. Repeat from * around, joining last ch to base of 1st r. Tie and cut. **3rd rnd:** R of 4 ds, join to any p on 2nd rnd, 4 ds, cl. * Rw, ch of (2 ds, p) twice, 2 ds. Rw, r of 4 ds, join to next p on previous rnd, 4 ds, cl. Repeat from * around, joining last ch to base of 1st r. Tie and cut. **4th rnd:** R of 4 ds, join to any p on 3rd rnd, 4 ds, cl. ** Rw, ch of (2 ds, p) 3 times, 2 ds. * Rw, r of 4 ds, join to next p on 3rd rnd, 4 ds, cl. Rw, ch of (2 ds, p) twice, 2 ds. Repeat from * 4 more times. Repeat from ** around. Fasten to base of 1st r. Tie and cut. **5th rnd:** R of 2 ds, join to any p on previous rnd, 2 ds, cl. * Sp of ¾ inch, r of 2 ds, join to next p on previous rnd, 2 ds, cl. Repeat from * around. Hereafter mark the end of each rnd. **6th rnd:** * Sp of ¾ inch, r of 2 ds, join to thread between next 2 r's on previous rnd, 2 ds, cl. Repeat from * around. **7th to 10th rnds incl:** Work same as 6th rnd, only making the sp between r's ¼ inch longer on each successive rnd. Tie and cut at end of 10th rnd. Starch and press.

Tatted Trio

MATERIALS: J. & P. Coats or Clark's O.N.T. Best Six Cord Mercerized Crochet, *Size 30, 3 balls of White or Ecru.*

Small doily measures 8 inches in diameter; large doily measures 10½ inches in diameter.

SMALL DOILY . . . 1st rnd: Make (r of 9 ds, p, 9 ds, cl) 4 times. Fasten to base of 1st r. Tie and cut. Tie ball and shuttle threads together. **2nd rnd:** R of 9 ds, join to p on r of 1st rnd, 9 ds, cl. * Rw, ch of 6 ds, (p, 4 ds) twice, p, 6 ds. Rw, r of 9 ds, join to same p on preceding r, 9 ds, cl. Rw, ch of 6 ds, (p, 4 ds) twice, p, 6 ds. Rw, r of 9 ds, join to p of next r, 9 ds, cl. Repeat from * around. Fasten to base of 1st r. Tie and cut. **3rd, 4th and 5th rnds:** Attach ball and shuttle threads to a p on previous rnd. * ch of 5 ds, p, 5 ds, join to next p on previous rnd (always join with shuttle thread). Repeat from * around. Fasten last ch where thread was attached. Tie and cut (24 loops). **6th rnd:** R of 6 ds, join to place where last rnd was started, 6 ds, cl. * Rw, ch of 3 ds, p, 3 ds, join to next p on previous rnd, (ch of 5 ds, p, 5 ds, join to next p on previous rnd) 3 times, ch of 3 ds, p, 3 ds. Rw, r of 6 ds, join between same ch and next ch, 6 ds, cl. Repeat from * around, ending with ch of 3 ds, p, 3 ds. Fasten to base of 1st r. Tie and cut. **7th rnd:** R of 6 ds, join to base of 1st r on last rnd, 6 ds, cl. * Rw, ch of 3 ds, p, 3 ds, join to next p on previous rnd, (ch of 5 ds, p, 5 ds, join to next p on previous rnd) 4 times, 3 ds, p, 3 ds. Rw, r of 6 ds, join to base of next r, 6 ds, cl. Repeat from * around, ending with ch of 3 ds, p, 3 ds. Fasten to base of 1st r. Tie and cut. **8th rnd:** R of 6 ds, join to base of 1st r on last rnd, 6 ds, cl. * Rw, ch of 3 ds, p, 3 ds, join to next p on previous rnd, (ch of 5 ds, p, 5 ds, join to next p of previous rnd) 5 times, ch of 3 ds, p, 3 ds. Rw, r of 6 ds, join to base of next r, 6 ds, cl. Repeat from * around, ending with ch of 3 ds, p, 3 ds. Fasten to base of 1st r. Tie and cut. **9th rnd:** R of 6 ds, join to base of 1st r on last rnd, 6 ds, cl. * Rw, ch of 5 ds, join to next p on previous rnd, (ch of 5 ds, p, 5 ds, join to next p on previous rnd) 6 times. Ch of 5 ds. Rw, r of 6 ds, join to base of next r, 6 ds, cl. Repeat from * around, ending with ch of 5 ds. Fasten to base of 1st r. **10th rnd:** * Ch of 5 ds. Rw, r of 6 ds, join between next 2 ch's on last rnd, 6 ds, cl. Rw, ch of 5 ds, join to next p on previous rnd, (ch of 5 ds, p, 5 ds, join to next p on previous rnd) 5 times, ch of 5 ds. Rw, r of 6 ds, join between same and next ch, 6 ds, cl. Rw, ch of 5 ds, join to base of next r. Repeat from * around, ending with ch of 5 ds. Fasten to base of 1st ch. Tie and cut.

11th rnd: Attach thread at base of 1st r of last rnd, * ch of 5 ds. Rw, r of 6 ds, join between next 2 ch's on last rnd, 6 ds cl. Rw, ch of 5 ds, join to next p, (ch of 5 ds, p, 5 ds, join to next p) 4 times, ch of 5 ds. Rw, r of 6 ds, join between next 2 ch's, 6 ds, cl. Rw, ch of 5 ds, join to base of next r, ch of 5 ds, p, skip 2 ch's, join to base of next r. Repeat from * around. Tie and cut. **12th rnd:** Attach thread to base of 1st r, * ch of 5 ds. Rw, r of 6 ds, join between next 2 ch's, 6 ds, cl. Rw, ch of 5 ds, join to next p, ch of 5 ds, p, 5 ds, join to next p, 5 ds, p, 3 ds. Rw, r of 6 ds, join between next 2 ch's, 6 ds, cl. Rw, ch of 3 ds, p, 5 ds, join to next p, ch of 5 ds, p, 5 ds, join to next p, ch of 5 ds. Rw, r of 6 ds, join between next 2 ch's, 6 ds, cl. Rw, ch of 5 ds, join to base of next r, ch of 5 ds, p, 5 ds, join to next p, ch of 5 ds, p, 5 ds, join to base of next r. Repeat from * around. Tie and cut. **13th rnd:** Attach thread to base of 1st r, * ch of 6 ds. Rw, r of 6 ds, join between next 2 ch's, 6 ds, cl. Rw, ch of 5 ds, join to next p, (ch of 5 ds, p, 5 ds, join to next p) 3 times, ch of 5 ds. Rw, r of 6 ds, join between next 2 ch's, 6 ds, cl. Rw, ch of 5 ds, join to base of next r, (ch of 5 ds, p, 5 ds, join to next p) twice, ch of 5 ds, p, 5 ds, join to base of next r. Repeat from * around. Tie and cut. **14th rnd:** Attach thread to base of 1st r, * ch of 5 ds. Rw, r of 6 ds, join between next 2 ch's, 6 ds, cl. Rw, ch of 5 ds, join to next p, (ch of 5 ds, p, 5 ds, join to next p) twice, ch of 5 ds. Rw, r of 6 ds, join between next 2 ch's, 6 ds, cl. Rw, ch of 5 ds, join to base of next r, (ch of 5 ds, p, 5 ds, join to next p) 3 times, ch of 5 ds, p, 5 ds, join to base of next r. Repeat from * around. Tie and cut. **15th rnd:** Attach thread to base of 1st r, * ch of 5 ds. Rw, r of 6 ds, join between next 2 ch's, 6 ds, cl. Rw, ch of 5 ds, join to next p, ch of 5 ds, p, 5 ds, join to next p, ch of 5 ds. Rw, r of 6 ds, join between next 2 ch's, 6 ds, cl. Rw, ch of 5 ds, join to base of next r; (ch of 5 ds, p, 5 ds, join to next p) 4 times, ch of 5 ds, p, 5 ds, fasten to base of next r. Repeat from * around. Tie and cut.

16th rnd: Attach thread to base of 1st r. * Ch of 5 ds. Rw, r of 6 ds, join between next 2 ch's, 6 ds, cl. Rw, ch of 5 ds, join to next p, ch of 5 ds. Rw, r of 6 ds, join between next 2 ch's, 6 ds, cl. Rw, ch of 5 ds, join to base of next r, (ch of 5 ds, p, 5 ds, join to next p) 5 times, ch of 5 ds, p, 5 ds, join to base of next r. Repeat from * around. Tie and cut. **17th rnd:** Attach thread to base of 1st r. * Ch of 5 ds. Rw, r of 6 ds, join between next 2 ch's, 6 ds, cl. Rw, ch of 5 ds, join to base of next r, (ch of 5 ds, p, 5 ds, join to next p) 3 times, ch of 5 ds. Rw, r of 6 ds, join between next 2 ch's, 6 ds, cl. Rw, ch of 5 ds, join to next p; (ch of 5 ds, p, 5 ds, join to next p) twice, ch of 5 ds, p, 5 ds, join to base of next r. Repeat from * around. Tie and cut. **18th rnd:** Attach thread to base of 1st r. * (Ch of 5 ds, p, 5 ds, join to next p) 3 times, ch of 5 ds. Rw, r of 6 ds, join between next 2 ch's, 6 ds, cl. Rw, ch of 5 ds, join to base of next r, ch of 5 ds. Rw, r of 6 ds, join between next 2 ch's, 6 ds, cl. Rw, ch of 5 ds, join to next p, (ch of 5 ds, p, 5 ds, join to next p) twice, ch of 5 ds, p, 5 ds, join to base of next r. Repeat from * around. Tie and cut. **19th rnd:** Attach thread to 1st p to right of end of last rnd; * (ch of 6 ds, p, 6 ds, join to next

p) twice, (ch of 6 ds, p, 6 ds, join to base of next r) twice, (ch of 6 ds, p, 6 ds, join to next p) 4 times. Repeat from * around. **20th rnd:** * Ch of 6 ds, join to next p, ch of 6 ds, join between next 2 ch's. Repeat from * around. Tie and cut.

LARGE DOILY . . . Same as Small Doily until 11th rnd is completed. **12th rnd:** Attach thread to base of 1st r of last rnd, * ch of 5 ds. Rw, r of 6 ds, join between next 2 ch's on last rnd, 6 ds, cl. Rw, ch of 5 ds, join to next p, (ch of 5 ds, p, 5 ds, join to next p) 3 times, ch of 5 ds. Rw, r of 6 ds, join between next 2 ch's, 6 ds, cl. Rw, ch of 5 ds, join to base of next r, ch of 5 ds, p, 5 ds, join to next p, ch of 5 ds, p, 5 ds, join to base of next r. Repeat from * around. Tie and cut. **13th rnd:** Attach thread to base of 1st r of last rnd, * ch of 5 ds. Rw, r of 6 ds, join between next 2 ch's, 6 ds, cl. Rw, ch of 5 ds, join to next p, (ch of 5 ds, p, 5 ds, join to next p) twice, ch of 5 ds. Rw, r of 6 ds, join between next 2 ch's, 6 ds, cl. Rw, ch of 5 ds, join to base of next r, ch of 5 ds, p, 5 ds, join to next p, ch of 5 ds. Rw, r of 6 ds, join between next 2 ch's, 6 ds, cl. Rw, ch of 5 ds, join to next p, ch of 5 ds, p, 5 ds, join to base of next r. Repeat from * around. Tie and cut.

14th rnd: Attach thread at base of 1st r, * ch of 5 ds. Rw, r of 6 ds, join between next 2 ch's, 6 ds, cl. Rw, ch of 5 ds, join to next p, ch of 5 ds, p, 5 ds, join to next p, ch of 5 ds. Rw, r of 6 ds, join between next 2 ch's, 6 ds, cl. Rw, ch of 5 ds, join to base of next r, ch of 5 ds, p, 5 ds, join to next p, ch of 5 ds. Rw, r of 6 ds, join between next 2 ch's, 6 ds, cl. Rw, ch of 5 ds, join to next p, ch of 5 ds, p, 5 ds, join to base of next r. Repeat from * around. Tie and cut. **15th rnd:** Attach thread at base of 1st r, * ch of 5 ds. Rw, r of 6 ds, join between next 2 ch's, 6 ds, cl. Rw, ch of 5 ds, join to next p, ch of 5 ds. Rw, r of 6 ds, join between next 2 ch's, 6 ds, cl. Rw, ch of 5 ds, join to base of next r, ch of 5 ds, p, 5 ds, join to next p, ch of 5 ds. Rw, r of 6 ds, join between next 2 ch's, 6 ds, cl. Rw, ch of 5 ds, join to base of next r, ch of 5 ds, p, 5 ds, join to base of next r, ch of 5 ds, p, 5 ds, join to base of next r. Rw, r of 6 ds, join between next 2 ch's, 6 ds, cl. Rw, ch of 5 ds, join to next p, ch of 5 ds, p, 5 ds, join to base of next r. Repeat from * around. Tie and cut. **16th rnd:** Attach thread at base of 1st r, * ch of 5 ds. Rw, r of 6 ds, join between next 2 ch's, 6 ds, cl. Rw, ch of 5 ds, join at base of next r, ch of 5 ds, p, 5 ds, join to next p, ch of 5 ds. Rw, r of 6 ds, join between next 2 ch's, 6 ds, cl. Rw, ch of 5 ds, join to base of next r, ch of 5 ds, p, 5 ds, join to next p, ch of 5 ds, p, 5 ds, join to base of next r. Rw, r of 6 ds, join between next 2 ch's, 6 ds, cl. Rw, ch of 5 ds, join to next p, ch of 5 ds, p, 5 ds, join to base of next r. Repeat from * around. Tie and cut.

17th rnd: Attach thread at base of 1st r, * ch of 5 ds, p, 5 ds, join to next p,

ch of 5 ds. Rw, r of 6 ds, join between next 2 ch's, 6 ds, cl. Rw, ch of 5 ds, join to base of next r, (ch of 5 ds, p, 5 ds, join to next p) twice, ch of 5 ds, p, 5 ds, join to base of next r, ch of 5 ds. Rw, r of 6 ds, join between next 2 ch's, 6 ds, cl. Rw, ch of 5 ds, join to next p, ch of 5 ds, p, 5 ds, join to base of next r. Repeat from * around. Tie and cut. **18th rnd:** Attach thread to 1st p to right of end of last rnd, * ch of 5 ds. Rw, r of 6 ds, join between next 2 ch's, 6 ds, cl. Rw, ch of 5 ds, join to base of next r, (ch of 5 ds, p, 5 ds, join to next p) 3 times, ch of 5 ds, p, 5 ds, join to base of next r, ch of 5 ds. Rw, r of 6 ds, join between next 2 ch's, 6 ds, cl. Rw, ch of 5 ds, join to next p, ch of 5 ds, p, 5 ds, join to next p. Repeat from * around. Tie and cut. **19th rnd:** R of 6 ds, join to end of previous rnd, 6 ds, cl. * Rw, ch of 5 ds, join to base of next r, (ch of 5 ds, p, 5 ds, join to next p) twice, ch of 5 ds, p, 3 ds. Rw, r of 6 ds, join between next 2 ch's, 6 ds, cl. Rw, ch of 3 ds, p, 5 ds, join to next p, ch of 5 ds, p, 5 ds, join to next p, ch of 5 ds, p, 5 ds, join to base of next r, ch of 5 ds. Rw, r of 6 ds, join between next 2 ch's, 6 ds, cl. Rw, ch of 5 ds, join to next p, ch of 5 ds. Rw, r of 6 ds, join to next p, 6 ds, cl. Repeat from * around. Do not cut. **20th rnd:** * (Ch

of 5 ds, p, 5 ds, join to next p) 6 times, ch of 5 ds, p, 5 ds, join to base of next r, ch of 5 ds. Rw, r of 6 ds, join between next 2 ch's, 6 ds, cl. Rw, ch of 5 ds, join to base of next r. Repeat from * around. Tie and cut. **21st rnd:** Attach thread at base of last r. * Ch of 5 ds, p, 5 ds, join to next p, ch of 3 ds, p, 3 ds. Rw, r of 6 ds, join between next 2 ch's, 6 ds, cl. Rw, ch of 3 ds, p, 3 ds, join to next p, (ch of 5 ds, p, 5 ds, join to next p) 4 times, ch of 3 ds, p, 3 ds. Rw, r of 6 ds, join between next 2 ch's, 6 ds, cl. Rw, ch of 3 ds, p, 3 ds, join to next p, ch of 5 ds, p, 5 ds, join to base of next r. Repeat from * around. Tie and cut. **22nd and 23rd rnds:** Attach thread to 1st p, * ch of 5 ds, p, 5 ds, join to next p. Repeat from * around. Tie and cut.

24th rnd: Attach thread to 1st p, * (ch of 5 ds, p, 5 ds, join to next p) 3 times, ch of 3 ds. Rw, r of 6 ds, join between next 2 ch's, 6 ds, cl. Rw, ch of 5 ds, join to next p, (ch of 5 ds, p, 5 ds, join to next p) 6 times. Repeat from * around. Tie and cut. **25th rnd:** Attach thread to 2nd p of last rnd, * ch of 5 ds, p, 5 ds, join to next p, ch of 5 ds. Rw, r of 6 ds, join between next 2 ch's, 6 ds, cl. Rw, ch of 5 ds, join to base of next r, ch of 5 ds. Rw, r of 6 ds, join between

next 2 ch's, 6 ds, cl. Rw, ch of 5 ds, join to next p, ch of 5 ds, p, 5 ds, join to next p, ch of 5 ds. Rw, r of 6 ds, join between next 2 ch's, 6 ds, cl. Rw, ch of 5 ds, join to next p, (ch of 5 ds, p, 5 ds, join to next p) 4 times, ch of 5 ds. Rw, r of 6 ds, join between next 2 ch's, 6 ds, cl. Rw, ch of 5 ds, join to next p. Repeat from * around. Tie and cut. **26th rnd:** Attach thread to 1st p, * (ch of 5 ds, p, 5 ds, join to base of next r) twice, ch of 5 ds, p, 5 ds, join to next p, ch of 5 ds. Rw, r of 6 ds, join between next 2 ch's, 6 ds, cl. Rw, ch of 5 ds, join to base of next r, ch of 5 ds. Rw, r of 6 ds, join between next 2 ch's, 6 ds, cl. Rw, ch of 5 ds, join to next p, (ch of 5 ds, p, 5 ds) 3 times, ch of 5 ds. Rw, r of 6 ds, join between next 2 ch's, 6 ds, cl. Rw, ch of 5 ds, join to base of next r, ch of 5 ds. Rw, r of 6 ds, join between next 2 ch's, 6 ds, cl. Rw, ch of 5 ds, join to next p. Repeat from * around. Tie and cut. **27th rnd:** Attach thread to 1st p, * (ch of 6 ds, p, 6 ds, join to next p) twice, (ch of 6 ds, p, 6 ds, join to base of next r) twice, (ch of 6 ds, p, 6 ds, join to next p) 3 times, (ch of 6 ds, p, 6 ds, join to base of next r) twice, ch of 6 ds, p, 6 ds, join to next p. Repeat from * around. Do not cut. **28th rnd:** Same as 20th rnd of Small Doily. Starch and press.

Honeymoon Breakfast

Materials Required—AMERICAN THREAD COMPANY "STAR" MERCERIZED CROCHET COTTON, ARTICLE 30, Size 50.

5—150 Yd. Balls White will make 2 Plate Mats and 2 Napkins.

1 Shuttle and 1 Ball.

4 Pieces of Linen 13 x 13 inches for 2 Napkins and 2 Table Mats.

Each Plate Mat measures about 12 x 20¾ inches.

HEMSTITCHING: Draw four threads from linen. Baste a ½ inch hem to the lower edge of open work. Fasten thread in hem to the left of work, * pick up a group of threads from right to left and draw threads together, take a stitch straight down into the hem, to the right of group picked up. Repeat from * across hem.

TABLE MAT: * R, 3 d, 2 p sep by 2 d, 3 d, p, 3 d, 2 p sep by 2 d, 3 d, cl r. Ch, 3 d, p, 3 d, 5 p sep by 2 d, 3 d, p, 3 d, join to center p of last r made. Repeat from * twice, * R, 3 d, 2 p sep by 2 d, 3 d, p, 3 d, 2 p sep by 2 d, 3 d, cl r, turn. Ch, 3 d, p, 3 d, 5 p sep by 2 d, 3 d, p, 3 d. Repeat from * 19 times. R, 3 d, 2 p sep by 2 d, 3 d, p, 3 d, 2 p sep by 2 d, 3 d, cl r. Ch, 3 d, p, 3 d, 5 p sep by 2 d, 3 d, p, 3 d, join to center p of last r made. R, 3 d, 2 p sep by 2 d, 3 d, p, 3 d, 2 p sep by 2 d, 3 d, cl r. Ch, 3 d, p, 3 d, 5 p sep by 2 d, 3 d, p, 3 d, join to center p of last r made. * R, 3 d, 2 p sep by 2 d, 3 d, p, 3 d, 2 p sep by 2 d, 3 d, cl r, turn. Ch, 3 d, p, 3 d, 2 p sep by 2 d, 2 d, join to center p of opposite ch, 2 d, 2 p sep by 2 d, 3 d, p, 3 d, join to center p of last r made. R, 3 d, 2 p sep by 2 d, 3 d, p, 3 d, 2 p sep by 2 d, 3 d, cl r, turn. Ch, 3 d, p, 3 d, 5 p sep by 2 d, 3 d, p, 3 d, join to center p of last r made. Repeat from * 17 times. R, 3 d, 2 p sep by 2 d, 3 d, p, 3 d, 2 p sep by 2 d, 3 d, cl r, turn. Ch, 3 d, p, 3 d, 2 p sep by 2 d, 2 d, join to center p of opposite ch, 2 d, 2 p sep by 2 d, 3 d, p, 3 d, join to center p of last r made.

Tie and cut.

2nd Strip. * R, 3 d, 2 p sep by 2 d, 3 d, p, 3 d, 2 p sep by 2 d, 3 d, cl r. Ch, 3 d, p, 3 d, 5 p sep by 2 d, 3 d, p, 3 d, join to center p of r just made. Repeat from *. R, 3 d, 2 p sep by 2 d, 3 d, p, 3 d, 2 p sep by 2 d, 3 d, cl r. * Ch, 3 d, p, 3 d, 2 p sep by 2 d, 2 d, join to center p of corresponding ch of 1 st strip, 2 d, 2 p sep by 2 d, 3 d, p, 3 d. R, 3 d, 2 p sep by 2 d, 3 d, p, 3 d, 2 p sep by 2 d, 3 d, cl r, turn. Ch, 3 d, p, 3 d, 5 p sep by 2 d, 3 d, p, 3 d, join to center p of r just made. R, 3 d, 2 p sep by 2 d, 3 d, p, 3 d, 2 p sep by 2 d, 3 d, cl r, turn. Repeat from * 19 times. * Ch, 3 d, p, 3 d, 5 p sep by 2 d, 3 d, p, 3 d, join to center p of r just made. R, 3 d, 2 p sep by 2 d, 3 d, p, 3 d, 2 p sep by 2 d, 3 d cl r.

Repeat from * turn, and complete strip same as 1st strip.

Work 2 more strips, joining all strips in same manner for each end of place mat. Sew to linen.

NAPKINS: R, 3 d, 2 p sep by 2 d, 3 d, p, 3 d, 2 p sep by 2 d, 3 d, cl r. * Ch, 3 d, p, 3 d, 5 p sep by 2 d, 3 d, p, 3 d, join to center p of last r made. R, 3 d, 2 p sep by 2 d, 3 d, p, 3 d, 2 p sep by 2 d, 3 d, cl r, turn. Repeat from * for length to go around napkins. Sew to napkin.

Delicate Doilies

MATERIALS: J. & P. Coats or Clark's O.N.T. Best Six Cord Mercerized Crochet, *Size 20, 2 balls of White.*

Round doilies measure about 8 inches in diameter; oval doily about 8 x 13 inches.

ROUND DOILY (Make 2) . . . STAR: Tie ball and shuttle threads together. R of 4 ds, lp, 4 ds, cl. * Rw, ch of 2 ds, p, 3 ds, p, 2 ds. Rw, r of 4 ds, cl. Repeat from * 3 more times. Rw, ch of 2 ds, p, 3 ds, p, 2 ds. Join to base of 1st r. Tie and cut. **1st rnd:** R of 4 ds, join to any p of Star, 4 ds, cl. * Rw, ch of 2 ds, p, 3 ds, lp, 2 ds. Rw, r of 4 ds, join to next p on Star, 4 ds, cl. Repeat from * around, joining last ch to base of 1st r. Tie and cut. **2nd rnd:** Repeat 1st rnd. **3rd rnd:** R of 2 ds, join to any p on previous rnd, 2 ds, cl. * Sp of ¾ inch, r of 2 ds, join to next p on previous rnd, 2 ds, cl. Repeat from * around. Hereafter mark the end of each rnd. **4th rnd:** * Sp of ¾ inch, r of 2 ds, join to thread between next

2 r's on previous rnd, 2 ds, cl. Repeat from * around. **5th to 9th rnds incl:** Work same as 4th rnd, only making the sp between r's ¼ inch longer on each successive rnd. **10th rnd:** * Sp of ¾ inch, r of 2 ds, p, 2 ds, cl, sp of ¾ inch, r of 2 ds, join to sp between next 2 r's on previous rnd, 2 ds, cl. Repeat from * around, ending with sp of ¾ inch, r of 2 ds, p, 2 ds, cl, sp of ¾ inch, join to 1st r. Tie and cut. Starch and press.

OVAL DOILY . . . 1st rnd: R of 4 ds, lp, 4 ds, cl. * Rw, ch of (2 ds, p) twice, 2 ds. Rw, r of 4 ds, join to lp of 1st r, 4 ds, cl. Repeat from * once more —end made. Work long side as follows: ** Rw, ch of 3 ds, p, 3 ds. Rw, r of 4 ds, p, 4 ds, cl. Repeat from ** 9 more times. Rw, ch of 3 ds, p, 3 ds. Make other end as follows: Rw, r of 4 ds, lp, 4 ds, cl. (Rw, ch of 2 ds, p, 2 ds, p, 2 ds; rw, r of 4 ds, join to lp of this end r, 4 ds, cl) twice. Work along opposite side as follows: Rw, ch of 3 ds, p, 3 ds. Rw, r of 4 ds, join to corresponding p on long side of oval, 4 ds, cl. Continue thus across, joining last ch to base of

1st r. Tie and cut. **2nd rnd:** R of 4 ds, join to 1st p on 1st ch of previous rnd, 4 ds, cl. Rw, ch of (2 ds, p) twice, 2 ds. Rw, r of 4 ds, join to next p on same ch, 4 ds, cl. Rw, ch of (2 ds, p) twice, 2 ds. Rw, r of 4 ds, join to 1st p on next ch, 4 ds, cl. Rw, ch of (2 ds, p) twice, 2 ds. Rw, r of 4 ds, join to next p on same ch, 4 ds, cl—end completed. * Rw, ch of 3 ds, p, 3 ds. Rw, r of 4 ds, join to p on next ch, 4 ds, cl. Repeat from * across to opposite end. Work other end and opposite side to correspond, joining last ch to base of 1st r. Tie and cut. **3rd rnd:** R of 4 ds, join to p on last ch of previous rnd, 4 ds, cl. * Rw, ch of (3 ds, p) twice, 3 ds. Rw, r of 4 ds, join to next free p, 4 ds, cl. Repeat from * 6 more times—end completed. ** Rw, ch of 4 ds, p, 4 ds. Rw, r of 4 ds, join to next p on previous rnd, 4 ds, cl. Repeat from ** across. Then work other end and opposite side to correspond, joining last ch to base of 1st r. Tie and cut. **4th rnd:** Repeat 3rd rnd of Round Doily. **5th to 12th rnds incl:** Repeat 4th rnd of Round Doily. **13th rnd:** Repeat 10th rnd of Round Doily.

Tray Mat Trim

MATERIALS: J. & P. Coats or Clark's O.N.T. Best Six Cord Mercerized Crochet, Size 30, 1 ball each of White and Color . . . A piece of white organdie, 13½ x 14½ inches . . . 2 pieces of colored organdie, each 5 x 13½ inches.

Tray Mat measures about 13 x 20 inches.

Make a narrow hem all around white organdie. Fold each piece of colored organdie in half lengthwise and machine stitch around raw edges, leaving a large enough space to allow for turning piece inside out. Turn and press, then turn under remaining raw edges and sew neatly. Use Color on shuttle and White on ball. Tie ball and shuttle threads together. * R of 6 ds, p, 6 ds, cl. Rw, ch of 4 ds, 3 p's sep by 4 ds, 4 ds. Rw, r of 6 ds, join to p of last r, 6 ds, cl. Rw, ch of 4 ds. Repeat from * until piece is 13 inches long, omitting the ch of 4 ds on last repeat. Continue along other side as follows: Ch of 4 ds, p, 4 ds. Rw, ** r of 6 ds, join to same p as opposite r's, 6 ds, cl. Rw, ch of 4 ds, 3 p's sep by 4 ds, 4 ds. Rw, r of 6 ds, join to same p as preceding r, 6 ds, cl. Rw, ch of 4 ds. Repeat from ** across, ending with ch of 4 ds, p, 4 ds. Tie at base of 1st r and cut. Make another piece like this. Sew tatting between white and colored organdie pieces by catching the center picot of each chain.

Flattering Collar

Materials: Clark's O.N.T. or J. & P. Coats Mercerized Crochet, size 60, 1 ball.
A shuttle.

1st rnd: This is the foundation row of rings and chains. R of 3 ds, 5 p's sep. by 3 ds, 3 ds, cl. * Make another r of 3 ds, 5 p's sep. by 3 ds, 3 ds, cl. Rw, ch of 3 ds, 4 p's sep. by 3 ds, 3 ds, rw. R of 5 ds, join to 3rd p of last r, 5 ds, p, 5 ds, p, 5 ds, cl. Rw, ch same as last ch. Rw, r of 3 ds, p, 3 ds, p, 3 ds, join to last p of last r, 3 ds, p, 3 ds, p, 3 ds, cl. Rw. Repeat from * for length required. After the last pair of picot r's, make a ch of 3 ds, 5 p's sep. by 3 ds, 3 ds, rw. R of 3 ds, p, 3 ds, join to 3rd p of last r, 3 ds, 3 p's sep. by 3 ds, 3 ds, cl. Rw, ch same as last ch. Rw, r of 3 ds, p, 3 ds, join to 4th p of last r, 3 ds, 3 p's sep. by 3 ds, 3 ds, cl. Rw. **2nd rnd:** The next ch worked on after the last r, starts 2nd rnd. Ch same as last ch. Rw. * Clover leaf of 3 ds, 3 p's sep. by 3 ds, 3 ds, join to last p of last r, 3 ds, 3 p's sep. by 3 ds, 3 ds, cl. 2nd r of 3 ds, join to last p of last r, 3 ds, 3 p's sep. by 3 ds, 3 ds, join to p of 1st round r of 1st rnd, 3 ds, 4 p's sep. by 3 ds, 3 ds, cl. 3rd r of 3 ds, join to last p of 2nd r, 3 ds, 6 p's sep. by 3 ds, 3 ds, cl. Rw, ch of 3 ds, 5 p's sep. by 3 ds, 3 ds, rw. R of 4 ds, join to 4th p of last r, 3 ds, 4 p's sep. by 3 ds, 4 ds, cl. Rw, ch same as last ch. Repeat from *, joining 2nd r's of all clovers to round r's of 1st rnd. At end, finish off to match beginning of rnd. **3rd rnd:** This is made of small round medallions joined to 2nd rnd. Starting at center, make r of 1 ds, 6 p's sep. by 3 ds, 2 ds, cl. Tie securely and cut off. R of 3 ds, p, 3 ds, p, 3 ds, join to one p of center r, 3 ds, p, 3 ds, p, 3 ds, cl. Rw, ch of 3 ds, 5 p's sep. by 3 ds, 3 ds, rw. * R of 3 ds, p, 3 ds, join to 2nd last p of last r, 3 ds, join to next p of center r, 3 ds, p, 3 ds, cl. Rw, ch of 3 ds, p, 3 ds, p, 3 ds, join to 3rd p of a ch of 2nd rnd, 3 ds, p, 3 ds, p, 3 ds, rw. R same as last r. Ch same as last ch, joining to 3rd p of next ch of 2nd rnd. R same as last r. Ch of 3 ds, 5 p's sep. by 3 ds, 3 ds. Make two more similar ch's and r's until there are six of each. Join the last r to 2nd p of first one,

Linen Doily

MATERIALS: J. & P. Coats or Clark's O.N.T. Best Six Cord Mercerized Crochet, Size 20, 1 ball of White or Ecru ... A hemmed linen circle, 7 inches in diameter.

Completed doily measures about 10 inches in diameter.

1st rnd: Tie ball and shuttle threads together. * R of 3 ds, 3 p's sep by 3 ds, 3 ds, cl. Rw, ch of 4 ds, 3 p's sep by 4 ds, 4 ds, rw. Repeat from * until there are 40 r's and 40 ch's. Join last ch to base of 1st r. Tie and cut. **2nd rnd:** R of 3 ds, 3 p's sep by 3 ds, 3 ds, cl. * Close to this, make r of 3 ds, 3 p's sep by 3 ds, 3 ds, cl. Rw, ch of 4 ds, p, 4 ds, join to center p of ch on 1st rnd, 4 ds, p, 4 ds, p, 6 ds. Rw, r of 3 ds, p, 3 ds, join to center p of adjacent r, 3 ds, p, 3 ds, cl. Rw, ch of 6 ds. Rw, r of 3 ds, 3 p's sep by 3 ds, 3 ds, cl. Rw, ch of 6 ds. Rw, r of 3 ds; 3 p's sep by 3 ds, 3 ds, cl. Rw, ch of 6 ds, join to last p of opposite ch, 4 ds, p, 4 ds, join to center p of next ch on 1st rnd, 4 ds, p, 4 ds. Rw, r of 3 ds, p, 3 ds, join to center p of adjacent r, 3 ds, p, 3 ds, cl. Repeat from * around, joining last ch to base of 1st r. Tie and cut. Sew to linen circle.

Flattering Collar

Continued from preceding page.

and fasten off last ch by joining into 1st r. Tie securely and cut off.

Second Medallion. Center r and 1st r as before. Ch of 3 ds, p, 3 ds, p, 3 ds, join to 3rd p of 4th ch of last medallion, 3 ds, p, 3 ds, p, 3 ds. Repeat from * of first medallion until all the medallions are worked.

4th rnd: Large clovers are now worked, to form foundations for scallops. **Clover Leaf:** 1st r of 3 ds, 3 p's sep. by 3 ds, 3 ds, join to 4th p of 2nd ch on outer side of a round medallion, 3 ds, 7 p's sep. by 3 ds, 4 ds, cl. 2nd r of 4 ds, join to 7th p of 1st r, 3 ds, 11 p's sep. by 3 ds, 4 ds, cl. 3rd r of 4 ds, join to last p of 2nd r, 3 ds, 6 p's sep. by 3 ds, 3 ds, join to 2nd p of 1st ch of next medallion, 3 ds, 3 p's sep. by 3 ds, 3 ds, cl. Tie securely and cut

off. Work similar clovers between all medallions.

Scallop Edging. * R of 3 ds, p, 3 ds, p, 3 ds, join to 3rd p of 1st r of 1st clover leaf, 3 ds, p, 3 ds, p, 3 ds, cl. Rw, ch of 3 ds, 4 p's sep. by 3 ds, 3 ds, rw. R of 3 ds, p, 3 ds, p, 3 ds, join to 4th p of 2nd r of clover, 4 ds, p, 4 ds, cl, rw. Ch of 3 ds, 3 p's sep. by 3 ds, 3 ds, rw. R of 4 ds, join to p of last r, 4 ds, join to next p of clover r, 3 ds, p, 3 ds, p, 3 ds, cl, rw. Ch of 3 ds, 7 p's sep. by 3 ds, 3 ds. Complete the rest of scallop to correspond. After last r of scallop, make a ch of 3 ds, p, 3 ds, rw. R of 3 ds, p, 3 ds, join to last p of ch of medallion just below, 3 ds, join to 1st p of next ch, 3 ds, p, 3 ds, cl. Rw, ch same as last ch. Repeat from * around. Tie securely and cut off.

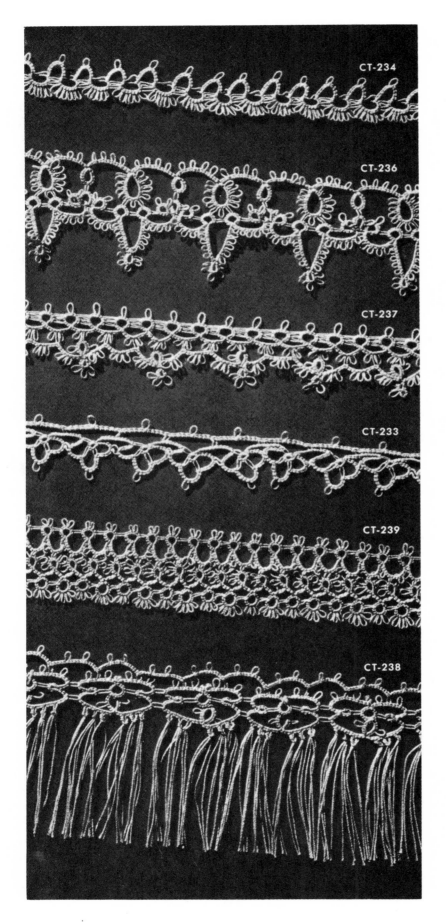

Still More Tatted Edgings

Sheer and Lovely

CT-234 . . . . Edging

MATERIALS: J. & P. COATS TATTING-CROCHET, *Size 70, 1 ball.*

Tie ball and shuttle threads together. R of (1 ds, p) 10 times, 1 ds, part cl. * Sp of ¼ inch. Rw, ch of 5 ds, p, 5 ds. Rw, r of 1 ds, join to last p of preceding r, 1 ds, join to next p of same r, (1 ds, p) 8 times, 1 ds, part cl. Repeat from * for length desired. Tie and cut.

CT-236 . . . . Edging

MATERIALS: J. & P. COATS TATTING-CROCHET, *Size 70.*

Tie ball and shuttle threads together. **1st row:** * Lr of (2 ds, p) 13 times, 2 ds, cl. Rw, ch of 3 ds, 4 p's sep by 3 ds, 3 ds. Rw, r of 8 ds, p, 8 ds, cl. Rw, ch as before. Repeat from * until piece measures slightly longer than length desired. Tie and cut. **2nd row:** R of 3 ds, p, * 3 ds, join to 6th p of lr of 1st row, 3 ds, p, 3 ds, cl. Rw, ch of 2 ds, 5 p's sep by 2 ds, 2 ds. Rw, sm r of (2 ds, p) 5 times, 2 ds, cl. Rw, ch as before. Rw, r of 3 ds, join to p of adjacent 3-p r, 3 ds, join to 8th p of same lr, 3 ds, p, 3 ds, cl. Rw, ch as before. Rw, r of 3 ds, join to p of preceding r, (3 ds, p) twice, 3 ds, cl. R of 3 ds, p, 3 ds, join to p of next r of 1st row, 3 ds, p, 3 ds, cl. R of (3 ds, p) 3 times, 3 ds, cl. Rw, ch as before. Rw, r of 3 ds, join to last p of preceding r. Repeat from * across. Tie and cut.

CT-237 . . . . Edging

MATERIALS: J. & P. COATS TATTING-CROCHET, *Size 70.*

Tie ball and shuttle threads together. **1st row:** R of 3 ds, 3 p's sep by 1 ds, 2 ds, p, 2 ds, 3 p's sep by 1 ds, 3 ds, cl. * Rw, ch of 3 ds, 3 p's sep by 1 ds, 3 ds. Rw, r of 3 ds, join to last p of previous r, (1 ds, join to next p of same r) twice; 2 ds, p, 2 ds, 3 p's sep by 1 ds, 3 ds, cl. Repeat from * for length desired. Tie and cut. **2nd row:** Fasten ball and shuttle threads to center p of first ch of 1st row. Ch of 3 ds, 3 p's sep by 1 ds, 3 ds, join to center p of next ch. * Ch of 3 ds, 3 p's sep by 1 ds, 3 ds. Rw, r of 3 ds, p, 3 ds, join to center p of next ch, 3 ds, p, 3 ds, cl. Rw, r of 3 ds, 3 p's sep by 1 ds, 3 ds, cl. (Ch as before and join to center p of next ch) twice. Repeat from * across. Tie and cut.

CT-233 . . . . Edging

MATERIALS: J. & P. Coats Tatting-Crochet, *Size 70.*

Tie ball and shuttle threads together. **1st row:** R of (2 ds, p) 3 times, 2 ds, cl. Rw, ch of 5 ds, p, 5 ds, join to last p of r, * (ch of 5 ds, p, 5 ds, join to next p of same r) twice. This constitutes a cluster. Rw, ch of 5 ds, p, 5 ds. R of (2 ds, p) 3 times, 2 ds, cl. Rw, ch of 5 ds, join to p of last ch of previous cluster, 5 ds, join to p of r. Repeat from * for length desired. Tie and cut. **2nd row:** Fasten ball and shuttle threads to p of first ch (between clusters) of 1st row. * Ch of 5 ds, p, 5 ds, join to p of next ch (between clusters). Repeat from * across. Tie and cut.

CT-239 . . . . Edging

MATERIALS: J. & P. Coats Tatting-Crochet, *Size 70, Yellow and Dark Lavender.*

Use Dark Lavender on shuttle and Yellow on ball. Tie ball and shuttle threads together. **1st row:** R of 4 ds, p, 2 ds, 2 p's sep by 1 ds, 2 ds, p, 4 ds, cl. * Rw, ch of 3 ds, 3 p's sep by 3 ds, 3 ds. Rw, r of 4 ds, join to last p of preceding r, 2 ds, 2 p's sep by 1 ds, 2 ds, p, 4 ds, cl. Repeat from * for length desired. Tie and cut. **2nd row:** R of 3 ds, 2 p's sep by 2 ds, 1 ds, join to center p of first ch of 1st row, 1 ds, 2 p's sep by 2 ds, 3 ds, cl (joining r made). Rw, ch of 3 ds. Rw, r of 3 ds, p, 3 ds, 3 p's sep by 1 ds, 3 ds, p, 3 ds, cl. * Rw, ch of 3 ds. Rw, make joining r as before and join to center p of next ch. Rw, ch of 3 ds. Rw, lr of 3 ds, join to last p of adjacent r, 3 ds, 5 p's sep by 1 ds, 3 ds, p, 3 ds, cl. Rw, ch of 3 ds. Rw, make joining r. Rw, ch of 3 ds. Rw, r of 3 ds, join to last p of lr, 3 ds, 3 p's sep by 1 ds, 3 ds, p, 3 ds, cl. Repeat from * across. Tie and cut.

CT-238 . . . . Edging

MATERIALS: J. & P. Coats Tatting-Crochet, *Size 70.*

Tie ball and shuttle threads together. **FIRST MOTIF . . .** Lr of (4 ds, p) 3 times, 4 ds, cl. Rw, ch of 3 ds, 4 p's sep by 3 ds, 3 ds. Rw, sm r of 3 ds, join to last p of lr, 3 ds, cl. Rw, ch as before. Rw, lr of 4 ds, p, 4 ds, join to center p of previous lr, 4 ds, p, 4 ds, cl. Rw, ch as before. Rw, sm r of 3 ds, join to free p of first lr, 3 ds, cl. Rw, ch as before. Join to base of first r. Tie and cut.

SECOND MOTIF . . . Work as for First Motif until 3 p's of first ch are made, 3 ds, join to corresponding p of adjacent ch of First Motif, 3 ds. Rw, sm r of 3 ds, join to last p of lr, 3 ds, cl. Rw, ch of 3 ds, join to corresponding p of adjacent ch of First Motif. Complete as for First Motif (no more joinings). Make necessary number of motifs, joining them as Second Motif was joined to First Motif.

HEADING . . . Fasten ball and shuttle threads to 3rd p of last ch of First Motif. * Ch of 5 ds, 2 p's sep by 5 ds, 5 ds, skip 2 p's, join to next p. Repeat from * across. Tie and cut.

FRINGE . . . Cut 2 strands of thread, each 3 inches long. Double these strands, thus forming a loop. Pull loop through a free picot on scalloped edge, then draw loose ends through loop. Pull up tightly. Make a fringe in each free picot across. Trim ends evenly.

Tatting Instructions

TATTING ABBREVIATIONS

R	. .	Ring	L P	.	Long Picot
L R	.	Large Ring	Ch	.	Chain
S R	.	Small Ring	Sp	.	Space
D	. .	Double or Doubles	Sep	.	Separate
P	. .	Picot	Cl	.	Close
S P	.	Short Picot			

TATTING

Tatting Shuttles are shaped like the *one illustrated.* Some are made with a hook at one end which is used to pull the thread through picots in joining. However, for a beginner the one without a hook is easier to manage as the hook hinders speed and is apt to be in the way. Instead of using the hook to pull the thread through in joining, a crochet hook or a pin may be used. For real dainty tatting use "STAR" Brand Tatting Cotton. It is made in white and a variety of beautiful colors. For heavier tatting use "STAR" Brand Mercerized Crochet Cotton sizes 20 to 50.

WINDING THE SHUTTLE

If the bobbin is removable and has a hole at one side, tie the thread and wind the bobbin until full. If bobbin is not removable wind thread around bobbin in center of shuttle but never allow thread to project beyond the shuttle.

The simplest form of tatting is the ring. This is made with one shuttle only. When making a design of chains and rings two shuttles or 1 ball and I shuttle are used.

When a design of rings worked with two colors is made. use 2 shuttles. While learning we suggest using "STAR" Brand Mercerized Crochet Cotton Size 20.

It must be remembered when learning to tat that the knot is made on the shuttle thread and not with it though all action is done with the shuttle thread. This is accomplished by easing the thread around fingers and pulling the shuttle thread taut.

DOUBLE STITCH

Unwind the shuttle so the thread is about 12 inches long. Hold the shuttle between the thumb and forefinger of right hand, with the thread coming from back of bobbin, take the end of thread between the thumb and forefinger of the left hand and pass it around the outstretched fingers, crossing it under the thumb. (Ill. No. 1.)

With the shuttle in your hand, pass the shuttle thread under and over the hand just below the point of fingers. Pass the shuttle between first and second fingers of the left hand, under shuttle and ring thread and bring it back over ring thread allowing the ring thread to fall slack by bringing the four fingers of the left hand together. (Ill. No. 2.) Pull shuttle thread taut and then spread the fingers of left hand till loop is close to fingers and thumb of left hand and pull tight. (Ill. No. 3.) The second half of the stitch is made in the opposite way. Allow the shuttle thread to fall slack, pass shuttle over ring thread and back under ring thread and over shuttle thread. (Ill. No. 4.) Pull shuttle thread taut and tighten ring thread until second half of stitch slips into place beside the first half. (Ill. No. 5.)

By pulling the shuttle thread, the stitch slips back and forth. If it does not, the stitch has been locked by a wrong motion and must be made over again. Practice the doubles until they can be done without looking at instructions. A picot is made by leaving a space between the stitches. (Ill. No. 6.)

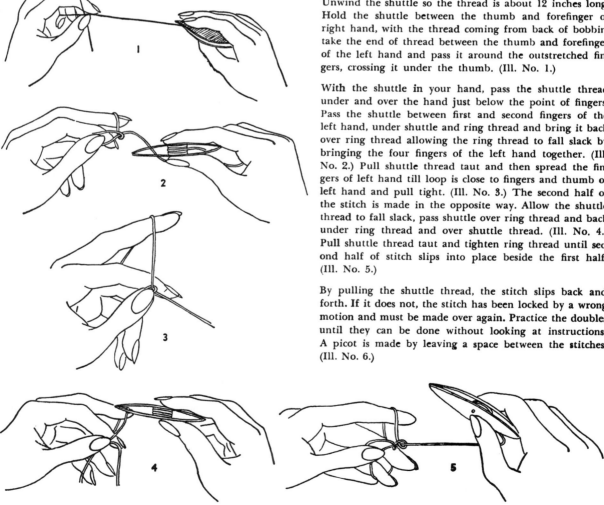

RINGS AND PICOTS

Make the first double as directed and work three more double stitches or doubles as they are usually termed.

PICOT. Make the first half of next double, slide it on thread stopping about ¼ inch from last stitch, complete the double and draw entire stitch in position next to doubles made. (Ill. No. 6 and 7.) Work doubles, then work another picot, work doubles, another picot and work doubles. Hold the stitches firmly in the left hand, draw the shuttle thread until the first and last stitches meet forming a ring. (Ill. No. 8.) For larger picots leave a larger space between doubles.

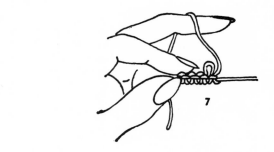

JOINING RINGS

Wind the thread around hand as for first ring and work first double stitch of next ring about ¼ of an inch from ring just made. Work three more doubles.

To join rings. If you are using a shuttle with one pointed end or a hook on one end, insert this end through the last picot of previous ring and pull thread through making a loop large enough to insert shuttle, draw shuttle through the loop and draw shuttle thread tight, this joins the rings and counts as the first half a double. (Ill. No. 9) complete the double, work 3 more doubles then a picot, 4 doubles, picot, 4 doubles, and close ring same as first ring. To reverse work, turn your work so that the base of ring just made is at the top and work next ring as usual.

To join threads. Always join thread at the base of last ring or chain by making a square knot and leaving the ends until work is finished as the strain of working may loosen the knot. Cut ends later. Never attach a new thread in ring as the knots will not pass through the double stitch.

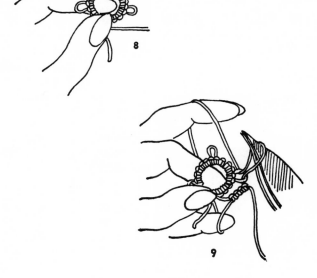

JOSEPHINE PICOTS

Single knots or Josephine picots. This is a series of single knots or just half of a double. Four or five knots for a small Josephine picot and 10 to 12 knots for a larger picot.

WORKING WITH A BALL AND SHUTTLE

All tatting designs containing chains and rings are made with one ball and a shuttle or two shuttles. To make a ring, the thread is wound to circle around the left hand and for the chain thread is wound half way around the hand. Tie the end of ball thread to end of shuttle thread. When you are making a ring use the shuttle thread, when ring is completed turn the ring so the base is held between the thumb and forefinger, place the ball thread over back of fingers winding it twice around little finger to control tension. (Ill. No. 10.) Work the chain over the ball thread using the shuttle thread. When chain is completed draw the stitches close together, drop the ball thread and with shuttle thread work another ring. Picots in chains are made and joined in same manner as in rings.

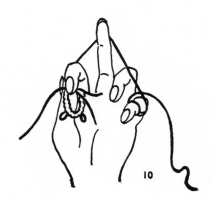

USING TWO COLORS

When two colors are used in making rings two shuttles must be used. If chains appear on the design with two colors use the second shuttle same as a ball.

Metric Conversion Chart

CONVERTING INCHES TO CENTIMETERS AND YARDS TO METERS

mm — millimeters   cm — centimeters   m — meters

INCHES INTO MILLIMETERS AND CENTIMETERS
(Slightly rounded off for convenience)

inches	mm		cm	inches	cm	inches	cm	inches	cm
⅛	3mm			5	12.5	21	53.5	38	96.5
¼	6mm			5½	14	22	56	39	99
⅜	10mm	or	1cm	6	15	23	58.5	40	101.5
½	13mm	or	1.3cm	7	18	24	61	41	104
⅝	15mm	or	1.5cm	8	20.5	25	63.5	42	106.5
¾	20mm	or	2cm	9	23	26	66	43	109
⅞	22mm	or	2.2cm	10	25.5	27	68.5	44	112
1	25mm	or	2.5cm	11	28	28	71	45	114.5
1¼	32mm	or	3.2cm	12	30.5	29	73.5	46	117
1½	38mm	or	3.8cm	13	33	30	76	47	119.5
1¾	45mm	or	4.5cm	14	35.5	31	79	48	122
2	50mm	or	5cm	15	38	32	81.5	49	124.5
2½	65mm	or	6.5cm	16	40.5	33	84	50	127
3	75mm	or	7.5cm	17	43	34	86.5		
3½	90mm	or	9cm	18	46	35	89		
4	100mm	or	10cm	19	48.5	36	91.5		
4½	115mm	or	11.5cm	20	51	37	94		

YARDS TO METERS
(Slightly rounded off for convenience)

yards	meters	yards	meters	yards	meters	yards	meters	yards	meters
⅛	0.15	2⅛	1.95	4⅛	3.80	6⅛	5.60	8⅛	7.45
¼	0.25	2¼	2.10	4¼	3.90	6¼	5.75	8¼	7.55
⅜	0.35	2⅜	2.20	4⅜	4.00	6⅜	5.85	8⅜	7.70
½	0.50	2½	2.30	4½	4.15	6½	5.95	8½	7.80
⅝	0.60	2⅝	2.40	4⅝	4.25	6⅝	6.10	8⅝	7.90
¾	0.70	2¾	2.55	4¾	4.35	6¾	6.20	8¾	8.00
⅞	0.80	2⅞	2.65	4⅞	4.50	6⅞	6.30	8⅞	8.15
1	0.95	3	2.75	5	4.60	7	6.40	9	8.25
1⅛	1.05	3⅛	2.90	5⅛	4.70	7⅛	6.55	9⅛	8.35
1¼	1.15	3¼	3.00	5¼	4.80	7¼	6.65	9¼	8.50
1⅜	1.30	3⅜	3.10	5⅜	4.95	7⅜	6.75	9⅜	8.60
1½	1.40	3½	3.20	5½	5.05	7½	6.90	9½	8.70
1⅝	1.50	3⅝	3.35	5⅝	5.15	7⅝	7.00	9⅝	8.80
1¾	1.60	3¾	3.45	5¾	5.30	7¾	7.10	9¾	8.95
1⅞	1.75	3⅞	3.55	5⅞	5.40	7⅞	7.20	9⅞	9.05
2	1.85	4	3.70	6	5.50	8	7.35	10	9.15

AVAILABLE FABRIC WIDTHS

25"	65cm	50"	127cm
27"	70cm	54"/56"	140cm
35"/36"	90cm	58"/60"	150cm
39"	100cm	68"/70"	175cm
44"/45"	115cm	72"	180cm
48"	122cm		

AVAILABLE ZIPPER LENGTHS

4"	10cm	10"	25cm	22"	55cm
5"	12cm	12"	30cm	24"	60cm
6"	15cm	14"	35cm	26"	65cm
7"	18cm	16"	40cm	28"	70cm
8"	20cm	18"	45cm	30"	75cm
9"	22cm	20"	50cm		

TRADITIONAL TATTING PATTERNS

Edited by Rita Weiss

Delicate but durable, tatting is an ideal needlecraft. It produces elegant heirloom lace that can be used and laundered repeatedly and will last long enough to actually become an heirloom. Since patterns are based on so few different stitches, tatting is simple to learn and easy to do once the stitches have been mastered.

This volume is a superb collection of more than 50 traditional tatting designs from rare thread company leaflets of the 1930s and 1940s. There are instructions for tatted doilies and edgings—a score of each—and tablecloths, place mats, adorable baby caps, bibs and bootees, classic collars, exquisite tatted yokes for slips or nightgowns and more—projects large and small enough to match your tatting experience and needs.

Beginners will find step-by-step instructions on how to wind and work with the shuttle and make all of the stitches necessary to complete the projects. For those who already know how to tat, *Traditional Tatting Patterns* is an excellent source of beautiful and enduring designs—a unique and useful addition to your needlework library.

Original (1986) Dover publication. Introduction. Instructions. Metric conversion chart. 33 black-and-white photographs. 10 black-and-white line illustrations. 48pp. 8¼ × 11. Paperbound.

ALSO AVAILABLE

ANNE ORR'S CLASSIC TATTING PATTERNS, Anne Orr. 32pp. 8¼ × 11. 24897-6 Pa. $2.50
TATTING PATTERNS, Julia E. Sanders. 48pp. 8¼ × 11. 23554-8 Pa. $2.95
TATTING DOILIES AND EDGINGS, edited by Rita Weiss. 48pp. 8¼ × 11. 24051-7 Pa. $2.95
TATTING: TECHNIQUE AND HISTORY, Elgiva Nicholls. 144pp. 6½ × 9¼. 24612-4 Pa. $4.95

Cover design by Paul E. Kennedy

IN USA

ISBN 0-486-250

9 780486 250663

T2-EVP-144

PRETTY FAMOUS TALES
ALADDIN AND HIS WONDERFUL LAMP
THE ELVES & THE SHOEMAKER, KING MIDAS, LITTLE RED RIDING HOOD

Love
from
kush